**DO NOT REMOVE
CARDS FROM POCKET**

arco pet library

Caring for Your Cat

William Thatcher
and
A. Windsor-Richards

Revised and Expanded
by Mario Migliorini

New York

HERE IS THE complete answer to every aspect of cat care, either for a novice about to acquire his first kitten or for a lifetime cat owner. Whether your problem is how to select a healthy kitten, diagnose feline illness, or breed aristocratic bluebloods, the answer will be found in this book. It is a book which no true cat-lover should be without.

Published by ARCO PUBLISHING COMPANY, INC.
219 Park Avenue South, New York, N. Y. 10003

Copyright © Arco Publishing Co. Inc., 1971

Certain portions of this book are © W. & G. Foyle Ltd., 1966

Library of Congress Catalog Number 71–126564
ISBN 0–668–02378–3

Printed in U.S.A.

CONTENTS

CHAPTER ONE

A CAT BY YOUR FIREPLACE

So YOU HAVE decided to become a cat-owner and enjoy the companionship of a cat by your fireplace.

What a picture this conjures in the mind, the sleek well-fed pet asleep before a blazing fire on a freezing, wintry night, or stretched out and relaxed on a summer's eve, after a day spent basking in the sunshine. Very pleasant and restful, and synonymous with quiet contentment and the peace of mind which all of us seek in one way or another.

To begin with, you tell yourself, there will be the charming, frolicsome kitten to captivate and amuse you all the hours of the day; not for several months will the little creature reach maturity, by which time a deep sense of understanding will have sprung up between you. So far so good. But before you hurry away to collect your new pet, I beg you to pause a moment and ask yourself if you really want it—yes, want it—and if you realize the responsibilities and disadvantages in becoming a cat-owner.

If everyone about to acquire a cat or kitten would give the idea careful forethought—in particular those who have never owned one before—there would be fewer unhappy, unwanted pets and less disappointed owners.

It is so easy—and very human too—to be swept away by blind enthusiasm at the sight of an innocent, wide-eyed kitten in need of a home, and then later in the cold light of reason to acknowledge one has made a mistake, has been too hasty, and isn't really keen on having a kitten at all.

Unless you are prepared to give it the time and attention

to ensure its well-being, it is wiser to recognize one's momentary enthusiasm for what it is, and decide against having a pet.

Having bought this book with the idea of learning something about cat care, the foregoing may sound discouraging, but quite frankly I mean it to be. It is so important to know what you are letting yourself in for, and I want to explain the disadvantages to you as simply as I can. Let me make clear that in particular these words are written for the new, prospective cat-owner; those with experience of keeping them will need no advice from me.

Without a doubt, cats are not everyone's pets; a true remark which has been made dozens of times. A dog will go to almost any lengths to win your approval, not so a cat. But— given understanding and affection it will return them a hundredfold all the days of its life.

Having grown up in a house full of cats, and later in adulthood bred them for some twenty years, I know this to be a fact.

I'm always amazed at the cat-owners—owners, mark you, not cat-lovers—who unashamedly admit that their pets are incredibly dull and show no interest in them whatever. (Having made the owner's acquaintance, I can applaud the cat's good sense!) "They don't do anything," they complain, "just eat and sleep all the time."

At this point I launch into the attack, explaining that if their pet is treated as an inanimate object and ignored, then obviously they won't get any response from it. Never receiving affection, it can't be blamed for not showing any.

Unhappily, I have seen far too many cats which fall into this category, and always I find it acutely distressing. Treated like doormats, they have no chance to show and develop the endearing characteristics inherent in all cats, and because of their owner's selfishness and lack of imagination, sadly they become "doormats" through no fault of their own.

None of this need have happened if these people had considered their cats in relation to themselves, instead of simply themselves in relation to their cats.

To the undecided would-be cat-owner several disadvantages will present themselves right away. For instance, unless trained when young to do otherwise, most cats play havoc with furniture by sharpening their claws on it, and a favorite chair or the new damask curtains may soon be ripped to ribbons. The alternative is to provide a scratching block or post, about which more is written in Chapter 4.

Next on the list, or possibly sharing first place with the problem of claw-sharpening, is the question of house-training. This often gives the housewife some anxious moments when she thinks about the new living room carpet, particularly if her husband doesn't like cats anyway. However, most cats are scrupulously clean creatures and quickly learn to use a litter tray (see Chapter 4).

Then there is the problem of your vacation. Your cat should not be left to fend for itself in your absence. Either leave it with a reliable friend or neighbor—and I stress the word "reliable"—or place it in a boarding establishment. There are many excellent establishments throughout the country, some providing separate chalets with wired-in runs, plus infrared lamps, etc., and these are usually the most satisfactory. Charges are not exorbitant for the service given. Details of those situated within a reasonable distance from your home can usually be obtained from the Yellow Pages of your telephone book.

You will be sure to be asked for a vet's certificate stating that your pet is in a healthy condition and that it has been inoculated against Feline Infectious Enteritis.

At this point you may decide it is all too complicated, and that anyway, any kitten you acquired would never become house-trained ("the carpet is *ruined*!") and that it would certainly turn up its nose at a scratching block ("I knew it wouldn't use one"), and would destroy your new suite of furniture in the shortest possible time. Then there are the added problems of feeding costs and possible vet's bills, to say nothing of the expense of its holiday home; none of which dawned on you when you decided to have a kitten. The bills are mounting before your eyes. "Can a cat really make such excessive demands?" you ask yourself gravely, to which I reply, "Yes, if it is to be cared for in the correct way." If you can't do this, I hope you won't make a decision which will bring unhappiness to yourself and the cat—particularly to the cat.

Having done my best to deter the half-hearted prospective cat-owners—cat-lovers will have stiffened at my derogatory remarks and in imagination have added two or three more to their feline families—let me now mention a few of the advantages of cat-keeping.

These are many and would fill pages and pages, far outweighing the disadvantages. Alley cat, Siamese, Blue Longhair or any other type—it makes little difference which you choose—all are extremely intelligent. The Siamese will prove more talkative than most, but all cats will respond to your words if you will take the trouble to speak to them. Over the years, my own experience with them has been very rewarding, and I never cease to wonder at their extraordinary ability to sense what is expected of them. Our cats live as members of the family (they are never mollycoddled or overfed), are treated with respect and given their rightful place. Because I spend so much time with them, they have learned that certain words mean different things and always surprise me by anticipating what I'm about to do next, be it gardening, painting, or anything else; off they rush ahead of me to make sure they miss nothing, and remain with me until the job in hand is finished.

It is the same when I am writing in my study; my young blue-pointed Siamese, "Francesca," will sit on my typewriter and do her best to prevent me working. When I explain this is serious business, she soon curls up on my lap and is fast asleep (which means keeping my knees pressed agonizingly together for hours on end lest she falls through).

There: suddenly "Francesca" has woken from her siesta and sits on my typewriter again protesting loudly that I must stop work at once as it's for -fifteen and time for our tea.

Tea over and typing once re, I am hoping that these words of mine will convince the cat-doubters among you to

keep a few goldfish instead. Think of it—little or no respon-
sibility, no cat hairs anywhere, the furniture unscathed, and
your new carpet impeccable and unblemished; dear reader,
you will live in a trim and orderly house. But without a cat
to beguile you every day, if you will pardon my saying so,
you will not have a home at all.

CHAPTER TWO

CHOOSING YOUR KITTEN

HAVING MADE up your mind to get yourself a kitten, you now have to decide whether it is to be a mongrel or pedigree. If you don't intend showing and simply want a pet, then it makes little difference which you decide to keep. Mongrel kittens are just as delightful as their blue-blooded relatives, though for some people a pedigree animal is infinitely preferable. Nine to ten weeks of age is a good time to acquire your kitten, because by then it will be weaned and house-trained. The actual business of acquiring a mongrel or pedigree may vary quite a lot, so I will deal with both in turn.

If you decide on a mongrel or alley cat, as they are often termed, in all probability it will come from one of three sources: it will be given to you by someone whose cat is forever producing large litters, or you will have been captivated by a ball of fluff peering at you from the window of a pet shop, or it will be a stray that has wandered in from the street.

In the first instance (without appearing to "look a gift horse in the mouth"), make certain it is full of lively good health, that its eyes are bright and clear, ears are clean, and mouth a healthy pink.

When buying from a pet shop, choose a reputable one; when in doubt, your local A.S.P.C.A. will advise you.

As well as checking the points listed above, see that the kitten is not pot-bellied, for this can mean the presence of worms. The coat should have a healthy appearance and not harbor flea-dirt or fleas, and there should be no sores or scabs on the skin. Your pet shop kitten will probably cost no more than ten dollars or so. If it's a stray, get your vet to examine it before you do anything else.

Presuming, however, that you want a pedigree kitten, then my advice is always to contact a breeder. If you don't know where to find one, your local veterinarian or A.S.P.C.A. may be able to help, but failing these sources, visit a cat show and contact a breeder there, or get a copy of *Cats Magazine,* 2900 Jefferson Avenue, Washington, Pennsylvania 15301, which lists cat breeders in the columns of its advertisers.

Your visit to the breeder will be full of interest, for apart from choosing your kitten, you will be able to see the whole litter as well as their dam. Once they are used to your presence, they will usually settle down and begin to play, and it won't be long before one is clambering up onto your lap. Take my advice—this is your kitten. While you have been trying to make up your mind which to choose, your kitten has chosen for you!

Do remember to take a basket or box with you in which to carry home your new pet, together with a small blanket if the weather is cold. Remember, he is about to be separated from his dam and brothers and sisters, and anything you can do to make him comfortable will help to minimize his initial distress.

Now, having paid for your kitten and been handed his diet sheet, pedigree form, and certificates of registration and inoculation (if he hasn't been inoculated, see your vet as soon as possible about having this done), you are all ready to start the journey home.

En route he may cry a good deal, so talk softly to him and do your best to quiet his fears. However, some kittens turn a deaf ear to kindly words when yelling for their mother, and you may have to take him from his basket and pacify him inside your coat. Do be careful; kittens can be as slippery as eels when they feel like it, and yours may decide that he's not going to return home with you after all.

I remember once seeing an enraged Siamese streaking

from the upper deck of an English bus when his owner had unwisely decided to let him play on the seat beside her. Luckily he didn't get very far. If you do take your kitten from his basket, keep firm hold of him, and if you are doubtful about it, leave him where he is. Better to be safe than sorry, and if the kitten is warm and comfortable, in all probability he will soon fall asleep.

When you go out of the house with your cat, such as to the vet, it is almost essential to put your kitten in a pet carrier. He will feel more secure while in an unfamiliar place. These pet carriers are available at your pet center in a wide range of prices.

CHAPTER THREE

YOUR KITTEN AT HOME

ON ARRIVAL HOME the first thing to be done is to show the kitten where you intend to keep his litter tray. Probably he won't be interested in it at first—after all, a great deal has happened to him in a short space of time—but place him in it three or four times, then let him explore the room, keeping an eye on him all the while.

Don't give him the run of the house right away; it will only confuse him, and he'll probably hide away in an inaccessible spot and you'll have some anxious moments trying to find him. Let him explore one room thoroughly, and when he's done this to his satisfaction, he'll probably use his litter tray and then settle down to wash himself. You can obtain litter trays from your local pet center or supermarket at the same time you buy cat litter. An aerosol can of litter deodorant might be a wise investment. For those who prefer to improvise, a baking pan or small plastic bowl works equally well, and garden peat can be used to replace regular litter. Never use sawdust because it may get in his eyes, or soil or sand because neither are really very satisfactory.

Incidentally, if you have children, do see to it that they are not forever picking up or playing with the kitten, particularly during his first hours in your home, when he should be left to himself, though not by himself. Explain that he is a baby, and like all babies, he must be treated with great care. Time for games later on, when a romp with a feather or table Ping-Pong ball will do no harm, though he must be allowed to sleep undisturbed as soon as he is tired.

Well—having washed himself, your kitten may now be interested in a little cooked chicken, some chopped raw beef, or a saucer of warm milk. However, never feed him milk and solid food together. When giving milk, see how he reacts to it, as it is inclined to be loosening. If his motions become loose, adjust his milk intake accordingly. If you can supply goat's milk for the kitten, so much the better; it is far superior in every way to cow's milk, and does not throw a strain on tiny digestions. An equal amount of evaporated milk and water is often well-tolerated, but contrary to popular belief, all cats do *not* like milk. Some hate it! Do remember at all times not to overfeed; about one to one and a half tablespoonsful of food should be ample for a growing kitten of six to seven weeks and upwards. As he matures, decrease the number of meals and gradually increase the quantity. At nine months he should be having two meals a day—one morning, one evening.

Those of you who buy a pedigree kitten will doubtless be given a diet sheet by the breeder. Do stick to it rigorously, because a sudden change of diet can easily upset a kitten. For those with a mongrel kitten, a diet sheet may not have been forthcoming, so remember to ask how it has been fed and try to give it similar food. For those who like a feeding chart at hand, the following may prove helpful.

To maintain normal good health, kittens require about 125 calories per pound of body weight, adults around 75 calories, and older cats 60 calories or less. Cats also require anywhere from 30% to 70% more protein than dogs, a high-fat diet, and ample Vitamin E. Those who intend to feed mostly canned food should be aware of the fact that cats are known to have become so addicted to the taste of tuna that they refused to eat another diet. Cats fed exclusively on tuna are known to develop a disease called Steatitis, which is believed to stem from the lack of Vitamin E in tuna. In the light of this information, tuna should be fed only on a restricted basis, and then only brands which say "Vitamin E added" on the label.

DIET CHART

(for kittens of 6 and 7 weeks and upwards)

Morning	Steamed fish, or fish cooked in milk. Take care to remove all bones.
Noon	Pablum, or similar baby food, made with evaporated milk or half-and-half.
Afternoon	Finely chopped chicken or scraped raw beef.
Night	Cooked chicken, beef, or fish. Specialized Pet Diet #5 (for cats), various Junior baby foods such as eggs, beef, liver, etc. Make useful additions or substitutes.

As a nightcap, give the kitten some warm milk to settle him for sleep. A drop or two of halibut oil each day on food is an invaluable addition to the diet, and a crushed theralin VMP tablet provides essential supplements.

By the way, remember to see that your kitten has access to fresh water at all times. Don't make the all-too-common mistake of thinking that milk will quench his thirst—it won't. Milk is a food.

To turn for a moment to the question of canned food for cats, let me say at once that I consider many of the brands on sale today to be first-rate and an invaluable addition to your cat's diet. However, I don't believe they should be fed day after day, as quite obviously they cannot take the place of fresh food.

Most kittens are usually house-trained when they go to their new owner, but in case yours isn't, a little patience and understanding will soon have him using his tray. Unless he goes there of his own accord, place him in it shortly after eating or drinking, and always upon waking. Remember that whenever you want your kitten to learn something important, talk to him quietly, telling him how clever he is, and stroke him all the while. You will be surprised how quickly he will understand just what you want him to do.

As he gets older he may prefer to use a corner of the garden and desert his litter tray. However, don't discard it; put it down each night and whenever the weather is bad and he is forced to remain indoors. If you do this, there should be no accidents. By the way—and this is advice for the mongrel cat-owner, since no pedigree cat-owner in his right mind would do such a thing—never, never shut the cat out last thing at night. This is a bad, cruel practice which can bring untold misery to the animal, particularly in bad weather, to say nothing of the risk of his becoming involved in cat fights, resulting in scratched eyes, lacerated ears, and septic wounds. See that your cat is settled in his basket or favorite chair before you retire for the night; it's his rightful place, and you will have the satisfaction of knowing that he is safe and sound till morning.

The problem of claw-sharpening is one which should be dealt with as soon as possible after the kitten's introduction to your home. Within hours of his arrival, the little chap will probably be digging his claws into the arm of your favorite chair, or possibly even into your leg! The solution is early training on a scratching mat or post. From my own experience, I have found the former the more satisfactory; one point in its favor is that, being flat, it can be tucked away out of sight behind a chair or in the corner of the room. Prepare your mat or post before the kitten arrives so that you can begin teaching him to use it at once.

To make a scratching mat you need a piece of stout wood approximately three-quarters of an inch thick, twenty-one inches in length by ten inches wide. Onto this tack a piece of coconut matting or a piece of carpeting. To encourage your kitten to use his mat, place some catnip under the matting before you tack it in place. This is not essential, but it will greatly increase his interest in it. Now for training. This is simply a matter of placing him on it at frequent intervals and showing him how to dig in his claws. Very gently press his toes so that the claws are unsheathed, and show him what you want him to do. Most kittens get the hang of it very quickly and thoroughly enjoy using it. Breeding kittens as we do, our cats all use a scratching block from the time they are a few weeks old, copying their mother's actions on it as soon as they are able to toddle across the room.

For those who want to make a scratching post, you will need part of a slender tree trunk, about eight inches thick by twenty-one inches in length. It can be covered with coconut matting or not, as you think fit. The post should be firmly fixed in position in the room where it is not prominent. I have seen posts affixed to wooden bases, but they always seem top-heavy and liable to fall over whenever the cat starts to use them; to my mind, the scratching mat is by far the better of the two. When your cat or kitten becomes so destructive that its behavior is no longer tolerable, declawing may be a solution. Although it is an unpleasant surgical procedure and is opposed by many prominent cat-lovers, it is far less drastic than having an otherwise lovable pet destroyed. Your vet is best suited to advise you about it.

Now we come to the all-important business of having your pet inoculated against the most deadly of all feline diseases—Feline Infectious Enteritis.

Unless this has already been done, arrangements should be made with your vet as soon as possible. There are several excellent vaccines on the market which can be given to kittens when eight weeks old, with a second injection ten to fourteen days later. It is not my intention here to write at length on the disease (this is done in Chapter Six), but merely to impress upon you the urgency of seeing that your kitten is given his shots without delay. This will not automatically guarantee immunity, but it will give him a much better chance of surviving, should he be unlucky enough to contract it.

CHAPTER FOUR

NEUTERING AND SPAYING

IF THE KITTEN you have acquired is to be a household pet and not used for breeding, do look into the important question of having it neutered or spayed. Many people who own a male kitten are apt to forget the comparatively short time it takes for it to reach maturity, and before they realize it they have a "full" male on their hands (one which is not neutered) which is anxious to mate and is spraying everywhere. The smell from spraying is repellent, and the most ardent cat-lover is liable to view his pet with a jaundiced eye unless arrangements are quickly made for neutering (or castration). Actually, of course, he has no one but himself to blame, as all this should have been attended to months earlier, but people do forget and it does happen. Incidentally, if you have been unlucky enough to experience the unpleasantness resulting from spraying on walls, furniture, etc., oil of citronella on cotton dabbed onto these areas will swiftly remove the odor.

Similarly, how many owners have been horrified to notice the sudden increase in size of their female cat? Is it possible she is old enough to have kittens? It is indeed, and a closer look will tell you that her family is already on its way. Once again this should have been attended to earlier and spaying carried out.

A male kitten can be neutered when he is about twelve to sixteen weeks old, at which time the testicles descend from the abdomen, though personally I prefer to leave it longer, to give his character a chance to develop, and also because it is my experience that males which are neutered at five to six months old are less likely to suffer the bladder troubles which sometimes attack in later years than those which were neutered at a very early age.

Until he is six months old the neutering may be carried out without an anaesthetic. Kittens suffer no ill-effects from neutering, and are soon bounding about again with their usual energy and enthusiasm. Neutered males make the most charming and devoted pets and really settle down as one of the family. Diet must always be watched, however; they do tend to put on weight after they have been neutered. Make certain you don't overfeed and see they have sufficient exercise.

Female cats come into season fairly frequently, though it varies from cat to cat, but unless mated they will become thin and nervous, and in some cases downright bad-tempered. Spaying is the answer, and it can be performed at the age of eleven weeks. Though a somewhat bigger operation than neutering, this should not decide the owner against it. With the advances in modern surgery in recent years there is little risk attached to it; in the operation itself the reproductive organs are removed.

Our own spayed females have suffered no ill-effects whatever, and careful nursing, warmth, and quiet were all that was needed afterwards to bring them back to normal in a few days. Many people feel that spaying is cruel, arguing that all families should be allowed to have at least one litter before the operation is performed. I thoroughly agree with this point of view, and have always felt that it helps to round out the animal's character and personality. To my mind, there is a lack of maturity, a sense of unfulfillment apparent in the adult female that has never had kittens which I find hard to describe. Those who have owned such cats will know what I mean.

But whatever plans you may make for your kitten, do see to it that spaying or neutering is carried out. Don't leave it until you have an unwanted litter on your hands, or are the perplexed owner of a smelly, battle-scarred tom who is the terror of the neighborhood. If you have a kitten or expect to have one in the near future, do something about it now—have a word with your vet RIGHT AWAY.

A ruddy female Abyssinian, sextuple Grand Champion Nile's Meresa III. By septuple Gr. Ch. Coppertone The Wild One of Nile ex Gr. Ch. Selene's Meresa of Nile. Breeder-Owner, Maureen Nottingham.

Septuple Grand Champion Coppertone The Wild One of Nile, a ruddy Abyssinian male. By Gr. Ch. Beaver's Zorro of Arcadia ex Dbl. Gr. Ch. Zina of Arcadia. Owned by Maureen Nottingham.

An award-winning Albino Siamese female, Sr. Ch. Avio's Thei-Lesa. Owned and bred by Mrs. Thelma M. Harrington.

ACFA and CFA Grand Champion, Glen Orry's Quane, a black with white Manx female. Owners-Breeders, Misses Ruth and Ellen Carlson.

A Red Tabby male long-hair kitten, at top, sits quietly but atten-
tively. At the slightest excuse, bottom photo, the kitten will romp
and jump, showing off his natural athletic prowess.

CHAPTER FIVE

COMMON ILLNESSES

IN THIS CHAPTER will be found a list of some of the more common illnesses which are likely to affect felines. It should be stressed, however, that in no instance should the suggested treatment replace a visit to your veterinarian. The symptoms given in each individual ailment should be used to help recognize the disorder, and to decide whether home treatment is desirable and safe.

Cats succumb to illness very quickly, and when there is any doubt as to what is wrong, contact your vet immediately. Don't make the all too common mistake of "waiting to see how the cat is in the morning" before getting help. Waiting at such times can prove fatal; your cat may be past helping or even dead by that time.

A healthy cat will have a sleek, shining coat and bright, wide-awake eyes, but in illness the picture will quickly change. If the animal goes off its food or sits moping about the place; if it vomits or has diarrhea, don't take any chances. Call your vet.

When treatment has to be given, remember the importance of even warmth at all times. Giving medicine should present no difficulties, providing one goes about it in the right way. Be calm and quietly efficient and when possible, get someone to lend a hand; it is possible to manage alone, but it usually takes longer. Carefully open the cat's jaws with the thumb and the first or second finger of your left hand across the top of the cat's head, holding the jaw on each side.

With the right hand, open its mouth and insert the tablets to the back of the throat. Close the mouth and hold it firmly shut; gently stroke the throat in a downward direction until the cat swallows the tablets. If someone is assisting you, get him to press the cat's front paws firmly down onto whatever surface the animal is standing on. This will do much to minimize the swiping paws which in a flash can knock a pill or capsule from your hand and sometimes inflict a sizable wound as well.

Giving liquids with a spoon can be a messy business, and I avoid using them whenever possible; using a hypodermic syringe (minus the needle, of course) or an eyedropper is better in every way. The nozzle can be inserted in the side of the mouth, and the liquid administered almost without the cat being aware of it. When giving oil, it is always better to warm it first, particularly in cold weather when it may have thickened. Warm oil flows more freely and will be easily absorbed.

Abscesses

Can form on any area of the body and are usually caused by bites, scratches, fight wounds, etc., into which dirt has penetrated. Get your vet to give an antibiotic injection and bathe with hot saltwater—taking care that it is not so hot that it burns the cat. When the abscess has burst, drain away the pus; don't allow it to close up too soon or another will form. Plug with cotton to keep open.

Asthma

Is not a common complaint among cats, but does affect some older cats. Symptoms are a troublesome cough and quick breathing. Cats so affected should not be allowed outdoors in cold damp weather. A light diet is advisable, and the bowels should be kept open. Your vet will prescribe appropriate drugs for treatment.

Bad Breath

The cause can be stomach trouble, bad teeth, indigestion, or worms. Any tartar on the teeth should be removed by the vet. Neglect can cause inflammation of the gums and possibly an abscess.

Biliousness

Probably the result of something he found and ate when you weren't around. Diarrhea or constipation may be present. Do not feed for a day, then begin with a little fish. Allow plenty of boiled water to drink, for the animal will probably be thirsty.

Bites

A fight with another cat may result in puncture wounds in the skin. To prevent them from becoming infected, bathe as soon as possible in a mild solution of non-toxic disinfectant.

Bladder Troubles

If the animal strains when urinating, or if there is blood in it, get immediate veterinary advice. Inflammation of the bladder or cystitis may be present. Old male cats and neuters seem particularly prone to this trouble.

Broken Limbs

Shock can be a factor here. Keep the cat warm and as quiet as possible. An X-ray of the injured limb will have to be taken, and the bone set when the cat is under an anaesthetic. After the initial surprise of finding themselves partially encased in plaster, most cats quickly settle down and accept it with their usual equanimity.

Bronchitis

In bronchitis, immediate treatment is required, or pneumonia or pleurisy may develop. Symptoms are difficult breathing, a cough, refusal to eat, and dribbling. Keep the cat in a place that has warm, even temperature. Call your vet at once.

Burns

Keep a fire guard in front of the fire when you're out of the room, and there will be little risk of the cat suffering from burns. If burnt, however, cover area with white vaseline.

For acid burns, bathe with a solution of bicarbonate of soda. When burning is severe, shock will undoubtedly be present and the vet should be called in. Meanwhile, keep the patient warm and quiet.

Canker

Inflammation of the ears. If serious ear problems develop, it is often the fault of the owner's overlooking the simple rules of hygiene. Treating a bad inflammation is another job for your vet, but to prevent canker and fungus infections from developing in the first place, put a few drops of Ear-Rite into each ear once a week. This will also help control ear mites, which frequently cause irritation. Ear problems are signified by continual scratching and head shaking.

Cataracts

Signified by white hazy opacity of the lens of the eye. Accompanied by loss of vision, cataracts often coincide with diabetes and nephritis, and your vet should be consulted as soon as this abnormality becomes evident.

Catarrh

Inflammation of the nasal passages. The cat sneezes a good deal, but is not actually ill. Sometimes there is a clear, watery discharge from the nose, and if treated early, this can be cured. However, once a heavy, yellowish discharge begins, treatment is more difficult and it may develop into snuffles, a chronic catarrhal condition which is extremely hard to cure. See your vet.

Cat Influenza

Keep the cat warm at all costs. The animal will sneeze a good deal, and there will be coughing and discharge from the eyes and nose. Coax the patient to take strained beef until fit enough to take solid food again. Make sure the eyes and nose are kept free of discharge by cleaning frequently with cotton dipped in a mild solution of disinfectant.

Choking

Possibly caused by something lodged in the throat. May need manipulation to remove it. Do not delay. Wrap the cat in a thick towel to prevent struggling, and if you can get someone to help you so much the better. Try to remove the object with forceps; if this fails, call your vet. Failure to do so could result in the death of the animal. Sometimes cats choke after eating grass.

Coccidiosis

A highly infectious disease of the intestines, caused by a parasite. Known to affect dogs, birds, and rodents, it also occurs in cats and kittens. The motions will be very loose and vile-smelling, and blood may be present. Absolute cleanliness must be observed, and litter trays should be changed after each motion. Treatment with sulfonamide drugs will usually effect a cure.

Constipation

To prevent constipation, feed a varied diet and allow plenty of exercise. When present, give liver or sardines. A pleasant remedy for this ailment is Femalt.

Convulsions

Not common in adult cats, but kittens are sometimes affected when teething. Get your vet to suggest a sedative, and keep your kitten on a light diet. Fits can also be an indication of worms. Do not attempt to worm the kitten yourself. Have a fresh sample of stool checked by the vet to determine what type of worm infection the kitten has. Contrary to popular belief, if a cat does have worms, evidence of the fact is not always visible in the feces—except when examined under a microscope, which should be done periodically by a vet.

Diarrhea

Often caused by giving too much milk, incorrect feeding, or change of diet. Raw ground meat will usually correct the trouble. Give Kaopectate.

Dribbling

Can mean the presence of bad teeth or tartar in old cats. Some cats will dribble when given tablets or medicine, to rid themselves of the taste. If constant dribbling occurs, consult your vet.

Ears

See *Canker*.

Eczema

A nonspecific dermatitis allergy or other superficial skin irritation, generally of obscure origin. Usually not contagious. May require prolonged treatment under veterinary supervision. Theralin VMP tablets have been used successfully.

Eyes

Always give an indication of a cat's physical state of health. Clear, bright eyes mean a healthy animal. When the hard or third eyelid partly covers the eye, something is usually wrong. It also can be an indication of worms. In the case of young kittens whose eyes have just opened, there may be one or two with gummed-up eyes or one eye which will not open. Do not neglect! Bathe with boracic and a little warm water, and ask your vet to recommend an ophthalmic ointment.

Feline Infectious Enteritis (Cat Distemper)

A real scourge and the worst of all cat illnesses. Onset is sudden and rapid, with vomiting, loss of appetite, and weakness. The cat will sit crouched and miserable before a bowl of water, but will not drink. There is rapid loss of condition and dehydration. Vomit is frothy and greenish-yellow, and is usually followed by an evil-smelling diarrhea. Constipation may also occur. Do not attempt unaided home treatment; get your vet in at once. The progress of the disease is so swift that a cat may be dead within hours of the onset. The virus of the disease is minute, and being spore-covered, can live for months in a suitable atmosphere. It is airborne, and can also be carried on hands, clothes, envelopes, etc. If you lose a pet through the disease, do not acquire another for at least six months. As a wise precaution, all kittens should be inoculated. This can be done when a few weeks old, with the second injection two weeks later. Use of the

vaccine will not guarantee immunity, but if your pet is unlucky enough to contract Feline Infectious Enteritis, its
chances of recovery are much greater. I am a great believer
in giving "booster shots" at a year old, to help the cat safely
through the next twelve months, for the disease rarely attacks
cats over the age of two years.

To sum up—at the first signs of Feline Infectious Enteritis,
isolate the animal and contact your vet at once. Do not
attempt to feed, as the small intestine will be inflamed. Keep
the cat warm and comfortable until your vet has had a chance
to see it.

Fleas

Are more likely to affect cats living in the country than
those of the town. Constant scratching indicates that fleas
or other parasites are present. Examine the animal's coat
carefully—if small black grit-like particles are found, this is
flea's excreta—not eggs, as is often thought. Comb your pet
daily with a special flea comb and dust with flea powder of
any of the good proprietary brands on the market. Lambert-
Kay's Victory flea collar will help prevent further infestations.

Indigestion

Usually caused by rapid eating or overeating, causing flatu-
lence and sickness. Give milk of magnesia. If the condition
persists, consult your vet.

Jaundice

Caused when the gall bladder malfunctions and "bile"
enters the bloodstream. Do not attempt home treatment or
waste any time. Get to your vet at once.

Lice

Not often found on cats—when they are, they lay their
eggs on the coat of the animal, and are very small and gray
in color. Same treatment as for fleas.

Mange

Most contagious. Caused by parasites burrowing under
the skin. There are two kinds, Soreoptic Mange and Follicu-

lar Mange. The former is contagious to other animals and humans, and in cats chiefly affects the head, face, and neck. The cat scratches itself continually, the hair drops out, and sore, bare patches appear. Follicular Mange is less common, but more difficult to treat. Keeping strictly to the treatment advised by your vet will eventually effect a cure, but it is usually a long business.

Pneumonitis

A highly contagious, persistent disease causing internal inflammation, runny eyes and nose, sneezing weakness, loss of weight, and photophobia. Treatment includes antibiotic and antihistamine injections, and recovery rate exceeds 70%.

Poisoning

Always keep poisons out of a cat's reach and remember to replace caps on bottles, particularly those in the greenhouse or garage, where they are liable to be forgotten and then get knocked over and spilt on to the floor. Cats are extremely sensitive to many chemical products found in and around the home. Insecticides, paints and paint thinners, weed and vegetation killers, gasoline, antifreeze, D-Con, DDT, and Tar are but a few. These products may contain arsenic, chlordane malathion, Phenol, sevin, and warfarin. Either swallowing or prolonged bodily contact with these and other similar products can produce violent toxic reaction. Salivation, diarrhea and vomiting, bloody urine, fever, weakness, convulsions, and loss of reflexes are among the symptoms that could indicate poisoning. Keep "Unidote," a universal antidote, handy. Call the vet.

Rabies

Rabies is an infectious disease that can affect all animals. The virus is usually transmitted in the saliva of infected animals as the result of a bite, or by the contamination of an open wound. Contact with unbroken skin does not result in infection. Prolonged confinement with infected animals was recently demonstrated as another possible method of transmitting infection.

Inflammation of the brain and spinal cord affects the central nervous system, and soon after exposure death invariably occurs. The time lapse between infection and the onset of encephalitis varies with the site of contamination. The nearer to the brain it is, the more rapidly it develops. Rabies symptoms, which can be both vague and misleading, are rarely as dramatic as generally supposed. Affected animals may just stop eating or drinking, or seek seclusion. Abrupt personality changes may also occur. Other symptoms, equally related to less serious conditions, may also exist. Outbreaks of rabies in the United States have been reduced by considerably more than half during the past twenty years. In 1968, 3,591 incidents were recorded nationally. Of these, 542 cases involved domestic animals, of which 295 were uncontrolled dogs. Strays are often a contributing factor in such incidents.

Vaccinating both dogs and cats against the disease is a sound precaution. Unless you have ample reason to believe that your pet has been in contact with a rabid animal, there is no cause for anxiety. Also, it has been estimated that less than 25% of those people exposed to the virus are ever affected.

Ringworm

In most animals and in humans, ringworm is characterized by round or semi-round hairless lesions. Strangely enough, cats may carry this infection without such indication. A "country cure" is to hold a fairly large lump of ice in firm contact with the infected area for a full ten minutes. This unorthodox treatment really works. If you suspect ringworm, have your veterinarian check for fungus with a Wood's Lamp. He will no doubt prescribe something more scientific, such as Griseofulvin.

Snuffles

Breathing is thick and heavy; the nostrils become clogged. Keep mucus wiped from the nostrils. Snuffles sometimes appears after pneumonia or distemper or a head cold. It is always difficult to cure. Give good food and extra Vitamin A to build up the animal's constitution. Make regular use of a nasal spray or dropper to help keep the nasal passages clear.

Ticks

These bluish-gray parasites are bloodsuckers, which cling tenaciously to the cat's body by their head. Flea powder is useless. Dab the tick with rubbing alcohol. It will release its hold at once. Destroy immediately. Always remove with tweezers, taking care not to break the parasite or an abscess may result.

Vomiting

Usually means the cat has bolted its food or overeaten. White or frothy vomit may indicate indigestion or gastritis. Should vomiting continue, get veterinary advice without delay.

Cats are a constant source of pleasure and joy for their owners. A healthy, well-fed and well-groomed cat is one of the most beautiful of domestic animals.

British Blue.

Abyssinian Kittens.

Manx.

Smoke Persian.

Tortoiseshell and White.

Red Tabby Persian.

CHAPTER SIX

NURSING AND CONVALESCENCE

IT CANNOT BE denied that our much-loved pets sometimes make extremely difficult patients.

In nursing them through illness and the convalescence that followed, some of mine have been angelic, seeming to know that one was trying to help them over a difficult period; they took their pills and liquid medicine without fuss and ate the special tidbits and meals which had been prepared with such care. Then there are the others, the difficult ones who seem hell-bent on dying. One very autocratic lady tortoiseshell of mine was the worst patient I have ever known. In health she was gentle and loving, but once ill, she became stubborn and truculent, refusing all help to get her better. She would neither eat nor drink, and even if only slightly off-color, would lie down and roll her eyes upwards as if her last moment had come. Eventually, after much coaxing, she would usually allow a morsel of food to be placed in her mouth. It had to be small, however, and always breast of chicken. Her classic example of refusing to eat was some years ago, after she had been spayed. Latterly her litters had held no interest for her, and it was with great difficulty that we were able to make her feed them. During their births, she had wandered about the room dropping them here and there on the carpet, and then showed no further interest in them. It was then that we decided that her days of motherhood must come to an end.

The spaying operation was a success, and I collected her from the vet's on the evening of the day it was performed.

Back home, she was placed in her basket, away from the other cats, to recover in peace and quiet. Her progress was normal, but not, alas, her appetite, for she promptly went on a hunger strike. The vet called twice a day and was unable to explain her behavior; she had no fever, her temperature was normal. As the days passed, she grew thinner and thinner, refusing all the foods she would usually have swallowed in a moment.

I counteracted by making certain she had vitamin shots from the vet each day. Even so, she seemed disinterested in everything that was being done for her benefit; she simply lay back, wan and beautiful, as if she fancied herself a feline Camille, which I am sure she did.

On the sixth day, I could circle her stomach with my thumb and first finger; something had to be done pretty quickly if she was to be saved. But what? The vet suggested raw chicken giblets (minus bones). As she wouldn't eat cooked giblets, I held out little hope. However, it was worth a try. I spread a little chicken liver on my finger and dropped it into her mouth. Her face registered horror and disgust, and then, miracle of miracles, she actually swallowed it! Instantly I produced more, but the lady was not going to be hurried. She would eat (if she felt like it) in her own good time. But eat she did, albeit with an expression of long-suffering. From then on she never looked back.

By contrast, another female of mine was spayed one day, and on the next promptly and methodically removed the stitches herself. We had no trouble getting her to eat, and she was back to normal in next to no time.

I have given these two examples to show owners—particularly novice owners—how behavior in cats can vary, and how each one needs individual attention.

Two old alley-cat sisters I once owned were spayed and rather reluctant to start eating again, but their diffidence was quickly overcome by putting them on strained beef, a wonderful standby in illness which is usually relished by the patient.

To conclude this brief chapter, nursing and convalescence

mean little more than using common sense, giving regular attention to the cat, plus peace and quiet, together with a light tempting diet for a few days before returning to the usual food. As I have said, some cats can be difficult and frequently are, and it is then that willing the animal to recover together with unlimited patience must be brought into play.

A sick cat, feeling too poorly to lick itself, very often appreciates being smoothed with a cloth, which has been dipped in hot water and well-wrung.

CHAPTER SEVEN

THE BROOD QUEEN

THIS CHAPTER WILL have to be divided into two parts, dealing first with the alley cat and then the pedigree.

Although biologically the processes by which they become proud mothers is the same, the devious routes by which they can achieve this blissful state are not. To the alley-cat owner possibly the first indication he will have that his cat is with kitten will be her ever-increasing size. Prior to her mating, she may have rolled a little, cried more often, and been unusually affectionate, but unless he knew the signs of a cat in heat, he probably dismissed it as simply that she was growing more loving, or he may not have noticed anything at all.

Gestation period for a queen is sixty-three to sixty-five days but the litter's arrival can be a few days earlier or later without there being undue cause for alarm. However, she must be carefully watched during the last week or so of pregnancy, and if she appears at all unhappy or in obvious distress call your vet. Litters may vary from one to six kittens —there are seldom more; four is a good-sized family for any cat to manage. No cat—be she alley or pedigree—should be allowed to have more than two litters a year. This may be hard to arrange in the case of the mongrel who comes and goes at will, but the owner of the pedigree will be well aware of the marauding toms that lie in wait for the "calling" queen, and will either keep her shut in or send her off to be mated by a pedigree stud as soon as she is ready.

If the little alley cat seems bent on producing litter after litter, it is far kinder to have her spayed, to prevent her wearing herself out. So many unwanted mongrel kittens are produced year after year, and it is wrong to run the risk of adding to them. The ideal situation, I feel, is to let the cat have one litter and experience the satisfaction of motherhood, then to have her spayed.

As the cat grows rounder, don't panic and think she must be given more food right away. This is wrong. To do so could produce large kittens, which she may have difficulty in expelling, and it certainly won't improve her digestion. However, in the fourth week of pregnancy the amount of food must be increased. In the week the kittens are due to be born, it is important to give a small amount of olive oil every day. Vitamin D and calcium should be given—the two combined can be bought in tablet form at most drugstores—and a little should be sprinkled on the cat's food.

You will, I hope, have a kittening box all ready for the expected family. Show it to the cat a few days before they are due and try to get her used to the idea of sleeping in it. She may decide she doesn't like it, in which case keep an eye on her as kittening time draws near, for she's probably decided to have them in your bed! Line the box with plenty of dry newspapers and place it out of direct light—my cats always have their box at the bottom of a shoe closet. Most cats are well able to have their kittens unaided, but it's as well to be on hand in case something goes wrong and veterinary aid must be hastily summoned. Most of my own cats —past and present—have liked me to stay with them until the last kitten was safely delivered. Once the new family has all arrived, remove the soiled newspapers and replace them with a good thickness of fresh newspapers with a warm blanket on top. They will now settle down and snuggle near their mother, and if everything has gone according to nature's plan, there will be that look of blissful contentment on her face which tells you that though she loves you dearly, this is the happiest moment of her life. And that's your cue to leave her with her babies.

However, sometimes things don't go smoothly, and you may have to help the cat at such times. Always make sure your hands are freshly scrubbed and sterilized in case of an emergency. If you have to help in delivering the kittens, make absolutely certain that you get the afterbirth. A kit is born in a sac from which it must be quickly released or it will suffocate. The cord attached to the afterbirth must be severed—use bluntish scissors which have been boiled and sterilized, but don't cut too near the kitten's tummy. The afterbirth must be removed from the queen with great care; hold the cord firmly between thumb and finger of your left hand, not more than two inches from the kit's body. Rough pulling may cause the kit to have an umbilical hernia. Next, with thumb and finger of your right hand holding the cord, withdraw the afterbirth. As it comes away, move your finger forward so that you do not break the cord.

Kittens are often born quickly one after the other and the mother is unable to deal with them. If this happens, wipe any mucus from mouths and nostrils with a towel and place them on a well-covered hot-water bottle in a box until all are born, then return to the queen. It sometimes happens that a kitten will get wedged on its entry into the world. Quietly and quickly wrap a piece of cotton or a towel around the exposed portion of the kit's body. With great care and working in harmony with the queen, ease the kitten every time you feel her strain. Never, never attempt to pull out the kitten. If you are not successful in your attempts contact your vet immediately.

It sometimes happens, though fortunately not often, that a queen will be so unlucky that she will lose her entire litter. When this happens, her milk should clear without difficulty; if it doesn't, try a little Epsom Salts in her food. Should this fail to help her, once again it's time to call in the vet.

Now to pedigree queens. It matters little which breed you possess; they are all delightful. Having purchased a female kitten and become enchanted by her, you decide to breed some kittens of your own. Let us pretend you have a Burmese kitten—a most charming breed with a wonderful temperament, whose popularity is forging ahead in leaps and bounds. Having acquired your Burmese, the next step should be to join the Burmese Cat Club. For information write United Burmese Cat Fanciers, Mrs. Ralph M. Robie, 1811 Maux Drive, Houston, Texas 77043.

Once your kitten has become an adult, which will be at nine months, you can think about mating her. Some kits are precocious and "call" at only a few months old, but they should not be mated, for the strain of producing and rearing a family would certainly undermine their constitutions. I have only once mated a cat at less than nine months old—actually it was eight months at the time—and exhausted by incessant "calling." I sought veterinary advice and was advised to mate her, but to allow her only one or two kittens; she produced four and the others went to a foster-mother. Having selected the best possible stud for your queen (details of studs will be found in *Cats Magazine*, 2900 Jefferson Avenue, Washington, Pennsylvania 15301, mentioned earlier) arrange well in advance with the stud owner the day and time of her arrival; if you can take her there by car and collect her afterwards so much the better. If she travels by REA Express, make sure she has a comfortable shipping box; it should not be too small, or too large either, for she may slither about in it and hurt herself. See that the lid is firmly secured and the container itself has a Livestock label affixed to it.

CHAPTER EIGHT

REARING HEALTHY KITTENS

ONCE THE MOTHER CAT, whether pedigree or mongrel, has safely been delivered of her litter, the less she and her young ones are interfered with the better. A healthy mongrel dam should be able to rear six kittens quite comfortably, but if you are not sure of homes for them when they reach about two months of age, then it is far wiser to let her keep just one or two. This will not only benefit the dam, but also, naturally, the remaining one or two kittens.

If there are children in the house, try and persuade them to resist the temptation of peeping at mother and litter too often. Although cats have been domesticated for a very long time, the dam still retains the natural instinct to seek some quiet, dark retreat in which to rear her youngsters, and this desire for privacy should be respected. Until the kittens' eyes are open and they begin to explore a little, two or three visits a day by a responsible adult, to make sure all is well, should be quite sufficient. Animals are a great deal more sensitive than many people suppose, and females are more than normally sensitive, of course, when their young are not yet able to fend for themselves.

To rear healthy kittens then, quietness and peace are important for both mother and young. You would not think that interference could have any kind of reaction upon a new-born kitten, but it can. This was proved to me by a remarkable experience which I would not have believed had I not witnessed it myself. I was asked to examine a litter of mongrel kittens which were only two days old. I was to select two for the mother to rear and have the others destroyed. The dam had left the litter for a few minutes, and while I was looking at them, the owner's cocker spaniel put his head in the nursery box and sniffed at the tiny blind youngsters. He was merely being inquisitive in a friendly way, but incredibly, the new-born kittens recoiled and actually made spitting noises. Yet there was no such reaction when I or the owner handled them. This seemed to be proof of the amazing and sensitive instinct of fear that must have been with these sightless little creatures from the moment of birth.

When the two surviving kittens were able to run about and play, they soon overcame their fear of the dog and thoroughly enjoyed tormenting him. This story does seem to demonstrate the importance of gaining the confidence of your pet by very gentle treatment in the early stages. It is not a good thing to let children do any handling until the kittens are old enough to explore. It is inclined to worry the dam and probably upset the digestions of the youngsters.

Supposing you have had a kitten given you, or bought one from a breeder or a pet shop, the first thing again is to try and gain its confidence the moment it enters your home. You realize now how sensitive a kitten can be, and it is of paramount importance to keep it soothed and calm from the outset. Of course, kittens and grown cats vary in their temperaments, and some have more confidence than others. It will depend a lot how this new pet of yours has been treated before it came to you.

When the kitten, which should be at least two months old, first arrives at your home, pet it and talk to it soothingly before putting it down to explore this strange new world which is your lounge or kitchen. But make sure, if it seems nervous, that the fireplace is guarded and the windows and doors closed. Kittens have been known to rush straight up a chimney!

When the kittens are a few weeks old, the more they are handled by the children, so long as they are gentle, the better it is for future relationship. And the more they are encouraged to play and be active, the better it is. In every healthy young creature, whether it is a human child, a lamb, or a kitten, there is an instinct to race and romp and play. This is nature's way of strengthening limbs and muscles and building a healthy foundation for independent days to come.

It does not matter whether it is a pedigree kitten or a mongrel, one thing is certain, and that is that good food, good, draftless sleeping quarters, considerate handling, and in fact a really sound start in life, will breed a strong healthy pet which will be a delight to you for many years. I know at least one mongrel ginger cat who is over twenty years old. You can be sure he was well looked after as a kitten, and thereafter.

The question of food has already been discussed, and it need only be added that most cats have their likes and dislikes, and these should be studied. Try to vary the food as much as possible and use canned foods only as a standby or occasional change, not as a daily item on the menu. Most cats seem to enjoy chicken more than anything, and it is a good, natural food for them, so don't mind the extra trouble of cooking. But don't forget to remove the bones from your pet's ration.

Cats are very fastidious feeders, particularly the pedigree ones, so utensils should be strictly clean and the food fresh.

Fish hardly seems a natural food for feline creatures, yet most of them thoroughly enjoy it. I once owned a black mongrel female who was crazy about fish. There was a large lake close to the house and if she noticed that I went out with a rod in my hand she would insist on coming out in the boat with me. She had a disconcerting habit of walking round the inch-wide gunwale of the boat while I was rowing along trolling for trout. She fell in on a number of occasions. Within a few minutes of fishing her out, she, not in the least disconcerted, would be doing the same thing again. She could see better that way if I was reeling in a fish. It was always a miracle that she did not get hooked herself, for she would grab at my capture almost before it was in the boat.

Incidentally, this little black cat, called Sue, was born wild

Chinchilla.

Siamese.

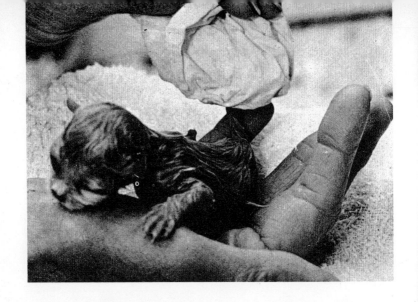

A new-born kitten, two minutes old. (From *The Arco Book of Cats* by Grace Pond, photo by Anne Cumbers.)

These kittens are just two weeks old.

A Brown Burmese kitten. (From *The Arco Book of Cats* by Grace Pond.)

An all-white Manx. (From *The Arco Book of Cats* by Grace Pond, photo by Anne Cumbers.)

in the woods. I found her mother in a rabbit snare and after freeing her (which was no easy task since she was mad with fright), I found Sue, who was about six weeks old, crying pitifully in a nearby bracken patch. I left her there all day in case the mother returned, but the old cat had been so frightened that she was not seen again. I kept Sue until her death ten years later. She would have probably lived many years longer, being fit and healthy, but she picked up some poison from somewhere, probably from catching a mouse or rat that had been poisoned.

I was as fond of that little cat as any pedigree one that I have owned. She was a real character and a wonder at catching rabbits. But she still loved her fish. If she missed seeing me go out with the rod, she was always waiting in the boathouse when I returned. She once ate thirty raw minnows which I had trapped for bait, and then looked around for more! So don't forget to vary your pet's diet with fish.

It is to be hoped that you have not been put off altogether from owning a kitten by the long list of ailments with which cats can be afflicted. There is no need to be. It is wise to read of these so that if certain symptoms occur, you will be able to recognize them and take early steps to combat the trouble. And if you follow the advice given in this book in regard to inoculation and feeding and general treatment, there is no reason why you should not have a pet that will be a companion and a pleasure to you for many years without, perhaps, having a single day's illness.

There is never any trouble in regard to games and exercise if there is more than one kitten, for they will get up to wonderful antics together. But, presuming you have decided to keep a kitten, you can always help it to amuse itself by providing a small ball; a Ping-Pong ball is excellent, because it is nice and light and easy for the very small kitten to cuff around. There is another thing which all young kittens seem to love and which provides them with endless entertainment —a fairly large cardboard box turned upside down on the floor which has a hole cut in it, like a kennel, just large enough for the kitten to enter. This toy seems to appeal to their primitive nature. It becomes a jungle den to them. In this, they can lurk like a lion or a panther, just waiting for someone to pass near so that they can leap out with an expression of utmost ferocity upon their faces.

CHAPTER NINE

GROOMING FOR ALL BREEDS

As FAR AS short-haired pet cats are concerned, it is hardly necessary to groom them every day. A good brushing and combing once or twice a week should be ample. If you intend to show your cat, however, it should be groomed at least once a day. For your short-haired pet use a soft brush, followed by the use of a comb. Buy a suitable comb from a pet shop and make sure the points of the teeth are not sharp. What you are trying to achieve with your grooming is removing loose, dead hairs from the cat's coat. A sharp comb will scratch the skin and perhaps uproot living hairs.

When the brushing and combing is done, it is a good idea to finish off by polishing the coat. Draw the palms of the hands smoothly from the direction of head to tail. A good sheen will be obtained by this treatment. For real perfection, say for showing, you can follow the example of the professionals and finish off with a piece of silk material.

It is obvious that a long-haired cat needs a great deal more attention, particularly if it has a free run of the garden. Once the coats get really matted, it is difficult to get them clean and smooth again. Only regular attention will keep them as they should be.

It is the usual practice to brush this type of fur the opposite way to which it naturally lies. The coats are so long and thick that to brush from head to tail results in shutting in a lot of the loose hairs. Do sections at a time and keep freeing the brush, or obviously you will be putting some of the hairs back instead of taking them all out. Brush against the grain from the tip of the tail to the head. The comb, however, should always follow the natural lie of the coat.

A stiffer bristled brush may be used for these cats. Special cat brushes are available from pet shops, and you will find that the best type for long coats has widely spaced bristles set in a rubber foundation.

Perhaps, during the early days of grooming, your cat will be restless and disapproving, but use patience, as always, and you will probably find that your pet will come to quite enjoy the process. If the cat obviously dislikes your first efforts with comb and brush, it is advisable to keep the operation brief to begin with, then gradually lengthen. It will become reconciled before long. Many cats seem to thoroughly enjoy the attention.

Remember to inspect the ears at frequent intervals. If they appear to need cleansing, sponge them with warm water. A pad of cotton wool is a good thing to use. Then dry carefully and dust with boracic powder. This is an excellent safeguard against canker. The corners of the eyes should also be sponged if anything has accumulated there.

If your cat should get thoroughly dirty, there is no reason why it should not be given a bath. If the water only comes about three inches up the cat's legs (so it won't panic) and it is not much more than body temperature, there will probably not be much opposition. Wet the fur thoroughly and then use a good quality shampoo.

After a good lathering and rinsing, it is important that the fur be completely dried with a towel. Pay particular attention to the areas between the legs.

Most cats dislike the sound of vacuum cleaners and hair driers, but if your pet does not object, then using the latter will save a lot of time and effort. So long as your cat is kept well-groomed, the question of a bath need not be considered except in the case of an emergency.

Another old trick for cleaning, and one which is not so objected to by the cat, is to rub in bran which has been dried in the oven in a baking pan. Rub it well into the coat by hand and then get rid of it by brushing.

The breeder, or the proprietor of your pet shop, will be only too pleased to show you the best sort of brush and comb to use for your particular yet. It is best to seek their advice if you are in any doubt, because by uprooting, you could do more harm than good by your grooming.

If you are the sort of person who has the time to spend on daily grooming and you like tending animals, then one of the long-haired varieties might suit you very well. It is always most rewarding to see how lovely and how healthy they look after a good grooming. If you have not the time to devote, then choose a short-haired cat, like a Siamese. They are very little trouble.

Personally, I would never deliberately acquire a mongrel cat. I have had several, and grown very fond of them, but they were wished on me—like Sue, the minnow-eater. No, I would always rather spend a few dollars on a pedigree kitten that I could be really proud of, than a few cents on a mongrel which might grow up to be quite unattractive. After all, you are going to possess your pet for years, so you may as well have something good, something that everyone will admire.

CHAPTER TEN

ALL KINDS OF CATS

I ENVY THOSE readers who have been persuaded (perhaps by this book) to take a kitten into their home, particularly those who have never kept one before, for they have endless interest, amusement, and companionship before them. As their kitten grows, they will be amazed at the speed and grace it displays. Just by watching the way the domestic cat walks and moves it can be clearly seen that it belongs to the same family as the lion, the leopard, the tiger, and the puma.

The real wild cat, as opposed to the domestic cat gone wild, still exists in the Scottish Highlands. Fossilized remains of this animal have been discovered, dating from the time when mammoths roamed the land. This cat is a great deal bigger than the domestic variety, and its tail is not tapered, but truncated and bushy. Its fur is a yellowish-gray color with handsome dark stripes. It is powerful enough to catch and kill hares, and even fawns and lambs. But this cat is not believed to be the ancestor of the domestic variety. There are two marked habits in which they differ. The true wild cat does not play with its victims before killing them, but dispatches them at once. Unlike the tame cat, it does not bury its droppings.

Once, when I was waiting in a hide for wood pigeons, I saw a mongrel black cat, which had been living wild in the woods for some months, catch a young rabbit. This one, although domesticated originally, did not play the "cat-and-mouse" game, but killed and began to eat at once. I suppose it depends on how hungry they are. Perhaps on another, better-fed, occasion it might not have been so hurried. I must confess I hate to see a cat torturing its prey so I always put the victim out of its misery, if I am able to do so.

But, of course, the cat is not being consciously cruel. A cat is no more cruel catching a bird than a bird is catching a butterfly or a worm. It is their nature, and they inherit instincts handed down through countless years. The cat keeping its captive alive is training itself to hunt the better and to anticipate every move that its prey is likely to make. It is the instinct for self-preservation. If cats had the power to reason, one could then say with truth that they were cruel. It is not a very flattering realization that we are the only species that is both consciously cruel and wantonly destructive.

There are a great many breeds of cats from which to choose, and it will probably be of help to give a few particulars about some of the pedigree varieties. They are divided into two classes, the long-haired and the short-haired.

Domestic short-haired cats can be strongly recommended as excellent pets and companions. They are very intelligent and nearly always gentle. They are also hardy. If they are looked after in the proper way, given the right food and comfortable quarters, they will provide their owners with many years of interest and companionship.

Books like this one can be of great help to the novice, but common sense is just as important. I am thinking at the moment of this question of turning out the cat at night. I have heard people excuse themselves for doing this on a bitter winter night by saying: "Well, cats are nocturnal anyway. And what about those that go wild and live in the woods in all weathers? They manage all right."

There's not much common sense there. A cat living "rough" gradually becomes acclimatized. He's not suddenly shot out of a heated room into the bitter cold. A pet door, such as the Flexport, is not a bad idea. It does at least give the animal a choice.

I am assuming for the purpose of this chapter that we are looking for the sort of cat you would like to own as a pet. At the same time, if you decided to become a breeder, any of the domestic short-hairs mentioned are an intriguing challenge as far as producing something in the top class for showing is concerned.

Among the long-haired cats, the white ones are always greatly admired for their beauty, and they always seem to look so clean. There are two recognized breeds: the blue-eyed and the orange-eyed. But probably the most popular of all the long-haired cats is the Blue Persian. Different shades of blue are acceptable for showing, but the fur must be of uniform color over each individual cat. The eyes should be orange or copper in color.

In the breeding of all show cats it is always of paramount importance to attain the color demanded and also to concentrate on the pureness of the coat of one-colored cats. Just as the Blacks should have no white hairs, both short-haired and long-haired Whites should be free of any taint of yellow. But this is all part of the challenge and makes the breeding of a winner all the more a pleasure and pride to the breeder. While mentioning the Whites, it is interesting to note that the ones with blue eyes, both short and long-haired, usually seem to be affected by deafness. Yet Whites with other colored eyes, such as orange, have normal hearing.

Among those termed "foreign," although some have been bred in this country for very many years, the Siamese are undoubtedly the most popular. They are classed as Seal-Pointed, Blue-Pointed, and Chocolate-Pointed. They are equally beautiful, and the charm of this breed is that human companionship is so important to them. They are almost dog-like in their devotion to their owners. They are full of fun and, owing to their light streamlined bodies, extremely agile and active.

Another very friendly member of the "foreigners" is the Burmese. These also make splendid pets and companions. They are a shining dark-brown in color.

For those readers who intend to breed the show cats, there are seven cat-fancier associations in the Uinted States and one in Canada. Information regarding shows and member-ship can be obtained by writing to the following persons:

American Cat Association, Inc.
Mrs. Susan Page Ferraez
11366 Camoloa Avenue
Lakeview Terrace,
California 91342

American Cat Fanciers
  Association
Mrs. Evelyn King
6103 SE 19th Avenue
Portland, Oregon 97202

Canadian Cat Association
Mr. Garnet Lamb
176 Delrex Blvd.
Georgetown, Ontario,
Canada

Cat Fanciers' Federation, Inc.
Mrs. A. W. Dickens
192 Cowbell Road
Willow Grove,
Pennsylvania 19090

Crown Cat Fanciers
  Association
Mrs. Katie Turner
Route 3, Box 347½
Huntsville, Alabama 35806

Independent Cat Federation
Mrs. Carolyn Alig
3512 East Milton Street
Pasadena, California 91107

National Cat Fanciers
  Association
Mrs. Frances Kosierowski
8219 Rosemont
Detroit, Michigan 48228

United Cat Federation, Inc.
Mr. Ed Bowers
1350 Taft Street
Lemon Grove,
California 92045

While the standards and show rules may vary, as may the number of breeds recognized, the aim of each of these organizations is basically the same: the welfare, promotion and improvement of pure-bred cats. The following standards, adopted by the N.C.F.A., are reproduced here as a sample.

BREEDS

ABYSSINIAN
BURMESE
DOMESTIC
  SHORTHAIR
MANX
PERSIAN

REX
RUSSIAN BLUE
SIAMESE
HAVANA BROWN
KORAT

CHAMPIONSHIP CLASSES FOR THE
FOLLOWING COLORS:

ABYSSINIAN:
   Ruddy
   Red

BURMESE:
   Seal Brown
   Champagne
   Blue

DOMESTIC SHORTHAIR AND MANX:

   Blue-Eyed White   Red Tabby
   Copper-Eyed White   Brown Tabby
   Odd-Eyed White   Silver Tabby
   Blue   Blue-Mackerel Tabby
   Black   Red-Mackerel Tabby
   Red   Brown-Mackerel Tabby
   Cream   Silver-Mackerel Tabby
   Chinchilla   Tortoiseshell and White
   Shaded Silver   Blue Cream
   Blue Smoke   Tortoiseshell
   Black Smoke   Parti Color
   Blue Tabby   Cream Tabby

PERSIANS:

   SOLID COLOR DIVISION: TABBY AND TORTY DIVISION:
   Blue-Eyed White   Red Tabby
   Copper-Eyed White   Peke-Faced Red Tabby
   Odd-Eyed White   Brown Tabby
   Blue   Silver Tabby
   Black   Tortoiseshell and White
   Red   Blue Cream
   Peke-Faced Red   Tortoiseshell
   Cream

HIMALAYAN DIVISION:
Frost Point
Blue Point
Chocolate Point
Seal Point
Red Point
Tortie Point

BALINESE DIVISION:
Frost Point
Blue Point
Chocolate Point
Seal Point
Red Point
Tortie Point

SILVER DIVISION:
Chinchilla Silver
Shaded Silver

Blue Smoke
Black Smoke

CAMEO DIVISION:
Shell Cameo   (Corresponding to Chinchilla)
Shaded Cameo   (Corresponding to Shaded Silver)
Smoked Cameo   (Corresponding to Black or Blue Smoke)
Cameo Tabby   (A pale ground color with deep heavy red
                   markings

RUSSIAN BLUE:
Solid Blue

HAVANA BROWN:
Havana Brown

KORAT:
Silver Blue

SIAMESE:
Frost Point
Blue Point
Chocolate Point
Seal Point
Red Point
Tortie Point
Albino

THE FOLLOWING CLASSES FOR EACH BREED:

NON-CHAMPION:
1. Male Kitten
2. Female Kitten
3. Neuter Kitten
4. Spay Kitten
5. Male Longhair Household Pet
6. Female Longhair Household Pet

NON-CHAMPION: (*Continued*)
  7. Neuter and Spay Longhair Household Pet
  8. Neuter and Spay Shorthair Household Pet
  9. Male Shorthair Household Pet
 10. Female Shorthair Household Pet
 11. Male of New Breed
 12. Female of New Breed

CHAMPIONSHIP CLASSES:
 13. Male Novice
 14. Male Open
 15. Male Champion
 16. Male Senior Champion
 17. Male Grand Champion
 18. Female Novice
 19. Female Open
 20. Female Champion
 21. Female Senior Champion
 22. Female Grand Champion
 23. Neuter Novice
 24. Neuter Open
 25. Neuter Champion
 26. Neuter Senior Champion
 27. Neuter Grand Champion
 28. Spay Novice
 29. Spay Open
 30. Spay Champion
 31. Spay Senior Champion
 32. Spay Grand Champion

RUDDY ABYSSINIAN STANDARD

HEAD: Head should be moderately long and pointed with width between the eyes. Center of nose should be brick tile red.

EARS: Ears should be alert, comparatively large, and broad at the base.

EYE SHAPE: The eye opening should be almond-shaped.

BODY: The Abyssinian should be medium in size, with body medium long and graceful, showing well-developed muscular strength.

OBJECTIONS: Small, dainty, slender build; short, cobby build; coarse or heavy boned.

TAIL: The tail should be fairly long, thick at the base, and tapering.

LEGS: Legs should be proportionately slim.

FEET: Feet should be small and round, and with black pads.

TEXTURE OF COAT: The coat should be dense and fine in texture.

The color should be ruddy brown, ticked with various shades of darker brown or black, two or three bands preferred to single ticking. A darker shading along the spine is allowed in an otherwise good specimen. Inside of forelegs and belly should be of a shade to harmonize well with the main color, the preference being given to orange-brown. Ears and tail should be tipped with dark brown or black.

UNDESIRABLE: Bars on head, face, legs, or tail, cut one to five points under ticking. Cut one to five points for white on throat or chest. Cut three points to five points for white belly spots.

EYE COLOR: The eyes should be brilliant and expressive and should be gold, hazel, or green; the more depth the better.

CONDITION: Hard and muscular with no indication of fat.

RED ABYSSINIAN STANDARD

COLOR: To be dark glowing red, distinctly ticked with chocolate brown, deeper shades of red preferred. Ears and tail to be tipped with chocolate brown. Paw pads pink, with chocolate brown in between toes, this color extending beyond the paws of the hind legs. Nose leather rosy pink. Body color in kittens usually lighter in color. Eye color gold, green, or hazel. Black pads or ANY black hair disqualify.

The body type, the head and ears, the eyes, the coat, and condition are the same as the ruddy Abyssinian.

SCALE OF POINTS

HEAD	10	TEXTURE OF COAT	5
EARS	5	BODY COLOR	15
EYE SHAPE	5	TICKLING	10
BODY	15	RUDDINESS OF BELLY	5
TAIL	5	EYE COLOR	5
LEGS	5	CONDITION AND BALANCE	10
FEET	5		
TOTAL POINTS ON TYPE	50	TOTAL POINTS	50

SEAL-BROWN BURMESE STANDARD

COLOR: The mature specimen should be a rich, warm sable; shading almost imperceptibly to a slightly lighter hue on the underparts, but otherwise without shadings or markings of any kind. Allowance should be made for lighter color and possible faint striping in adolescents and kittens. White spots or patches to disqualify.

BODY AND TAIL: Body medium in size, muscular in development, presenting a somewhat compact appearance. Allowance to be made for larger size in males. An ample, round chest, with back level from shoulder to tail. Legs well proportioned to body, with round feet. Tail to be straight, medium in length, and free from visible vertebral defects.

HEAD AND EARS: The head should be pleasingly rounded and without flat planes, whether viewed from front or side. Face should be full, with considerable breadth between the eyes: tapering slightly to a short, well-developed muzzle. In profile, there should be a visible nose break. Ears to be medium in size and set well apart on the rounded skull; alert, tilting slightly forward, broad at the base, and slightly rounded tips. Roundness of head 7 points. Full face with proper profile 8 points, breadth between the eyes 4 points, ear set and placement 6 points.

EYES: Set far apart with rounded aperture, with color ranging from yellow to gold, the greater depth and brilliance the better. Blue eyes to disqualify; green eyes a fault. Placement and shape 5 points, color 5 points.

COAT: Fine, glossy, satin-like in texture; very close-lying. Short 4 points, texture 4 points, close-lying 2 points.

CONDITION: Perfect physical condition, with excellent muscle tone. There should be no evidence of obesity, paunchiness, weakness or apathy.

DEFINITION: The overall impression of the ideal Burmese would be a cat of medium size and rich, solid color, with substantial bone structure, good muscular development and a surprise weight for its apparent size. This, together with its expressive eyes and sweet face, present a totally distinctive cat which is comparable to no other breed.

OBJECTIONS: Pale eye color, blue or odd eyes; tabby markings; white whether as scattered hairs or patches. Winners to be withheld from cats with bobbed, screw, kinked, or pom-pom tails.

CHAMPAGNE: The mature specimen should be a sound warm beige, shading to a pale gold-tan underside. The legs and tail to be the same shade as the hair on the back, not darker. Foot pads a warm pinkish tan. Nose leather light, warm brown. Slight darkening on ears and face permissible due to the extreme paleness of the animal, but lesser shading preferred. Cat overall to be as even a beige as possible. Faint barring on adolescents and kittens permissible. Definite leg gauntlets to disqualify.

BLUE: The mature specimen should be a rich, sound, even blue-gray of velvety texture, characterized by a high sheen on the coat, giving an illusion of iridescence. Underside slightly paler than back. Nose leather and foot pads are to be blue-gray. Faint striping permissible in adolescents and kittens. Undesirable: Bars, warm tone in coat.

SCALE OF POINTS

COLOR	25	EYES	10
BODY AND TAIL	25	COAT	10
HEAD AND EARS	25	CONDITION	5
		TOTAL POINTS	**100**

BURMESE STANDARD (Approved by United Burmese Cat Fanciers)

DOMESTIC SHORTHAIR STANDARD

HEAD: Broad between the ears; cheeks well-developed; face and nose medium short.

EARS: Ears medium in size, round at the tips, and not too large at the base.

EYE OPENING: The eye opening should be round.

BODY: The body should be well-knit and powerful, showing good depth and full chest.

TAIL: Tail length should be in proportion to the body, rather thick at the base, and tapering slightly towards the end. Tail carried almost level with the back.

LEGS AND FEET: Legs of good substance and in proportion to the body. Feet neat and well-rounded. Five toes in front and four behind. Withhold winners for extra toes.

COAT: Coat should be short, lustrous and of good texture.

COLOR: See Description of color and color patterns in the Persian Section and the Breeds Section.

EYE COLOR: The eye color shall conform to the requirements for coat color.

SCALE OF POINTS

HEAD	10	LEGS AND FEET	10
EARS	5	COAT	15
EYE OPENING	5	COLOR	25
BODY	15	EYE COLOR	5
TAIL	5	CONDITION	5
		TOTAL POINTS	**100**

MANX STANDARD

HEAD AND EARS: The head should be round with prominent cheeks. Nose should be slightly longer than the Domestic Shorthairs, but must not be inclined to snipishness. Ears should be rather wide at the base, tapering slightly to a point.

BODY: The body should be compact, with short back that arches from shoulders to haunches.

TAILLESSNESS: Taillessness must be absolute in a show specimen. There should be a hollow at the end of the backbone where, in the usual cat, the tail would begin. Sometimes there is a slight rise at the end of the backbone which should not be penalized if it is stationary, but if it is movable, it must be considered the first joint of the tail and therefore a stub, and winners must be withheld.

HEIGHT OF HINDQUARTERS: The back legs should be very long and the forelegs much shorter, giving the appearance of very high hindquarters. The legs should have substantial bone.

ROUNDNESS OF RUMP: The ideal would be as round as an orange.

DEPTH OF FLANK: The flanks should be of greater depth than in the Domestic Shorthair, adding much to the short, cobby appearance.

EYES: The eyes should be large, round, and full. The color of the eyes should conform to the requirements for the color of coat.

DOUBLE COAT: The coat should be soft, with a well-padded quality arising from the longer open outer coat and the thick close undercoat. The double coat gives the Manx the appearance of having a short spongy coat.

COLOR AND MARKINGS: All colors of Manx are recognized that are recognized for Domestic Shorthairs. Winners should not be withheld for white BUTTON and LOCKETS.

CONDITION: Good physical condition, being muscular with no indication of fat.

SCALE OF POINTS

HEAD AND EARS	10	DEPTH OF FLANK	10
BODY	10	EYES	5
TAILLESSNESS	15	DOUBLE COAT	10
HEIGHT OF HINDQUARTERS	10	COLOR AND MARKINGS	10
ROUNDNESS OF RUMP	10	CONDITION	10
		TOTAL POINTS	100

PERSIAN STANDARD

TYPE: The perfect cat should be cobby of body, low on the legs, deep in the chest, massive across the shoulders and rump, with a short, rounded middle. In size, the cat should be large or medium, but there should be no sacrifice of type for the sake of size.

HEAD: The head should be round and massive, with great breadth of skull, and well-set on a neck not too long.

EARS: Neat, round tipped, set wide apart and not too open at the base.

NOSE: Short, snub, and very broad.

CHEEKS: Full.

JAWS: Broad and extremely powerful.

EYES: Large, round, full, set far apart, and very brilliant, giving a sweet expression to the entire face.

TAIL: Short, carried without a curve and at an angle lower than the back, but not trailing when walking.

BACK: Level.

LEGS: Thick and strong, forelegs perfectly shaped and a very strong appearance.

PAWS: Large, round, and firm; toes carried close; five in front and four behind.

COAT: Long hair. The coat should show perfect physical condition. It should be very fine in texture; soft, glossy, full of life, should stand off from the body. It should be long all over the body, including the shoulders. The ruff should be extremely long and continue in a deep frill between the forelegs. Ear tufts, long, curved. Toe tufts long. Tail very full.

UNDESIRABLE: Rangy body, flat-chested, long-legged, too long tail, long-nosed, large ears, too pointed ears, eyes set bias or too close together, receding chin, light bone, a foxy face.

WHITE: Pure white, no colored hairs; eyes deep blue, odd-eyed, or copper.

BLACK: Dense black color, the blacker the better, giving the appearance of BLACK SATIN, sound to the roots, free from any tinge of rust on tips or smoke undercoat. Eyes copper.

BLUE: Color blue, not drab, lighter shade preferred, but type should not be sacrificed for lightness of color. Eyes brilliant copper.

RED: Deep, rich, clear, brilliant red without markings or ticking; lips and chin the same color as coat. Eyes copper.

PEKE-FACED RED (Persian only): Same as for solid red, but with a decided resemblance to the Pekingese Dog. The nose should be very short, with a distinct indentation between the eyes. A decided wrinkled muzzle preferred in the Peke-Faced cat.

CREAM: One level shade of cream, sound to the roots. Eyes brilliant copper.

CHINCHILLA: Undercoat should be a pure white; the coat on back, flanks, head and tail should be tipped with black to give the appearance of sparkling silver; the legs may be very slightly shaded with tipping, but chin, ear tufts, stomach, and chest must be pure white; any barring or brown or cream tinge is a serious fault. Eyes to be green. Rims of eyes, lips, and nose to be outlined with black. Center of nose to be a brick red. A cat that has made championship in the Chinchilla class may not be shown in the Shaded Silver Class.

SHADED SILVER: Shaded Silver should be pure unmarked Silver, shading down the sides, face, and tail from dark on the ridge to white on the chin, chest, belly, and under the tail; legs to be the same color as the face. The color effect to be much darker than the Chinchilla. Barring or brown tinge to be considered a fault. Eyes to be green. Rims of eyes, lips, and nose to be outlined with black. Center of nose to be brick red. Any cat that has won championship as a Shaded Silver may not be shown in the Chinchilla Class.

BLACK SMOKE: A Smoke cat should appear black, with white undercoat and black points and mask, light silvery frill and ear tufts. Eyes deep copper.

BLUE SMOKE: A Blue Smoke cat should appear blue, with white or blue-white undercoat, dark blue points and mask, and a white or blue-white frill and ear tufts. Eyes deep copper.

TABBY PATTERN: The Tabby cat should show good contrast between the pale ground color and the deep, heavy markings. Head barred, with frown marks extending between ears and down the neck to meet the BUTTERFLY on the shoulders, which divides the head lines from the spine lines. These spinals, or back markings, consist of a distinct wide dark center stripe, with stripes of ground color on either side; these in turn bordered by a second dark stripe, making three dark stripes down the back. The dark swirls on the cheeks and sides of the body shall make complete unbroken circles and shall be centered by a large spot surrounded by the ground color. Legs are evenly barred with bracelets coming to meet the body markings. Tail evenly barred. The belly should have the characteristic VEST BUTTONS, or rows of dark spots, in the color of the dense markings. OBJECTIONS: White spots, blurred and indistinct markings, light tail.

BROWN TABBY: The ground color, including lips and chin, should be a rich tawny brown, and the markings a dense, clearly defined black. Eyes should be deep copper.

SILVER TABBY: The ground color should be a pure pale silver, with decided jet black markings. The eyes should be green, but in an otherwise good specimen, copper or hazel eyes are allowed.

TORTOISESHELL and WHITE: The head, back, sides, and tail should be black and red and/or cream, in clearly defined and well-broken patches. The color should be in patches and not brindled. The legs, belly, throat, and nose should be white. It is desirable that one side of the face be orange, and one side red or cream. Eyes should be copper. OBJECTIONS: Tabby markings; color in white portion or white in colored portion.

BLUE CREAM: The two colors, clear blue and cream, should be well-divided and broken into patches that are bright and well-defined. A blaze preferred. Eyes should be copper. OBJECTIONS: Tabby markings; colors that are brindled instead of in patches; solid color on face, legs, and tail; white markings in coat.

TORTOISESHELL: Black and red and/or cream in bright, clearly defined and well-broken patches. The colors should be patched and not brindled. It is desirable for half the nose to be black and half red or cream, constituting what is known as a BLAZE. Eyes should be copper. OBJECTIONS: Tabby markings, solid black face, legs, and tail; white chin or other white markings.

STANDARDS

Judges Score—To apply to all LONGHAIR colors
except Himalayan and Balinese.

COLOR	25	TYPE (including shape, size,	
COAT	15	bone & length of tail)	20
CONDITION	10	COLOR OF EYES	10
HEAD (including size and			
shape of eyes)	20	TOTAL POINTS	100

In all Tabby and Tortie colors the 25 points allowed for color to be divided 15 for markings and 10 for color.

DOMESTIC SHORTHAIRS ONLY

BLUE, RED, BROWN, AND SILVER MACKEREL AND TICKED TABBIES shall conform to the same color specifications as for the respective colors of the conventional tabby pattern. The color pattern differs in the design of the markings. Instead of the swirls, circles, butterfly, and multiple spine stripes of the tabby, the Mackerel Tabby may have one spine line and vertical bands of the marking color on the sides.

CREAM TABBY: The ground color should be cream with dense, darker cream markings. Eyes should be copper.

PARTI-COLOR: Parti-Color cats may be of any two or more colors, with either spotted, patched, brindled, or mingled colors.

CAMEO PERSIAN STANDARD

CAMEO PERSIANS are shaded cats, the coat having hairs that shade from pale cream at the skin or light red at the tips. The eye color is copper; the eye rims and nose are reddish pink instead of black and brick red respectively.

The Cameo patterns duplicate those of the Silver Persians:

SHELL CAMEO (Corresponding to Chinchilla)

SHADED CAMEO (Corresponding to Shaded Silver)

SMOKE CAMEO (Corresponding to Black or Blue Smoke)

CAMEO TABBY (A pale-cream ground color with deep red markings)

SHELL CAMEO: The undercoat should be a pale cream, almost white. The coat on the back, flanks, head, and tail should be sufficiently tipped with red to give a delicate tinsel appearance. The legs and face may be very lightly shaded, but the chin, ear tufts, stomach, and chest should be pale cream without tipping. The eyes should be copper and the rims of eyes and nose leather a violet, toned pink. OBJECTIONS: Barring on face, legs, tail, and body.

SHADED CAMEO: The Shaded Cameo should be pure, unmarked red, shading gradually down the sides, face, and tail from dark on the ridge to whitish cream on the chin, chest, and belly and under the tail; the legs to be the same tone as the face. The general effect should be much redder than the Shell Cameo. The eyes should be copper and the rims of eyes and nose leather a violet, toned pink. OBJECTIONS: Barring on face, legs, tail, or body.

SMOKE CAMEO: A Smoke Cameo cat should appear deep cream or red, with cream or white undercoat, red or deep cream points and mask, with pale cream neck ruff and ear tufts. The eyes should be copper. OBJECTIONS: Tabby markings and pale eye color.

CAMEO TABBY: The ground color should be pale cream, with decided red markings. The eyes should be copper.

(Cameo standards approved by the
CAMEO CAT CLUB OF AMERICA)

HIMALAYAN STANDARD

GENERAL: In appearance, the Himalayan cat should resemble a Persian cat in type, conformation, and coat length and texture, while having the eye color, coat color, and color pattern of the Siamese cat. While the eye color, coat color, and color pattern of the Siamese cat must be retained, any similarity in type to the Siamese is to be considered incorrect and undesirable.

HEAD: Head should be broad and round, with great width between the ears. Jaws broad and powerful, with cheeks full and prominent. Face and nose short, with nose almost as broad as long. OBJECTIONS: Long, narrow head; long nose; thin muzzle; overshot or undershot jaw.

EARS: Small, round-tipped, and set wide apart. OBJECTIONS: Large pointed ears; ears slanting out from head or too close together.

BODY: Back should be short and level; the mid-section well-rounded. Neck short and powerful. OBJECTIONS: Narrow chest; long and thin neck.

TAIL: Tail short and straight, carried without a curve, not trailed when walking. OBJECTIONS: Long tapering tail; winners to be withheld for kinked tail.

LEGS AND FEET: Legs short, thick, and heavily boned. Feet large, round, and firm, with toes close together. Five toes in front, four in back. OBJECTIONS: Light boned; long legs; oval feet; bowed legs; separated toes.

EYE OPENING: Large, round, and full. OBJECTIONS: Small eyes, crossed-eyed; eyes slanted or close together.

EYE COLOR: Clear, brilliant, and blue; the deeper blue the better. OBJECTIONS: Any color other than blue.

COAT: Coat should be long, thick, and soft; glossy, full of life; should stand off from the body; long all over. The ruff should be full and continued in a frill between the forelegs. Ear furnishings and toe tufts long; tail plume full. Seasonal variations in coat shall be recognized. OBJECTIONS: Close and short fur.

BODY COLOR: (Tone and depth of color 5; shadings 5.) The body color should be even, with slightly darker shadings across the shoulders and back, shading gradually into lighter color on belly and chest. Darker coloring allowed for older cats; kittens generally lighter in color. OBJECTIONS: Uneven body color or shadings; dark spot on belly; tabby markings or ticked markings; shadings off standard color.

POINTS: (Depth and evenness of color 5; conformation 5.) Mask, ears, legs, feet, and tail clearly defined in darker shade. Mask and ears to be connected by tracings, except in kittens. Colors to be Seal, Blue, Chocolate, Frost, and Red, with appropriate body color as provided in the Siamese Standard. OBJECTIONS: Complete hood; light hairs in points; bars on tail.

CONDITION: Firm in flesh but not fat.

SCALE OF POINTS

HEAD	10	EYE COLOR	5
EARS	5	COAT	15
BODY	15	BODY COLOR	10
TAIL	5	POINTS	10
LEGS AND FEET	10	CONDITION	10
EYE OPENING	5	**TOTAL POINTS**	100

BALINESE

SCALE OF POINTS

BODY COLOR	10	EYES	5
POINT COLOR	15	COAT	20
TYPE (Body and Tail)	20	CONDITION	10
HEAD AND EARS	20	**TOTAL POINTS**	100

TYPE, COLOR: Same as for Siamese, except for length of coat; modified wedge allowed.

MUST be registered N.C.F.A. Foundation record (F3) to be eligible to be shown in championship class. SIX (6) generations Balinese to qualify for Studbook registration.

RUSSIAN BLUE STANDARD

GENERAL: The Russian Blue cat differs from the Blue Domestic Shorthair in being lithe, long, and svelte in type, having a shorter, finer-textured coat, more plushlike in texture.

HEAD: The skull should be flat and narrow; the forehead and neck long.

EARS: The ears should be rather large, wide at the base, with very little inside furnishings. The skin of the ear is thin, rather transparent, and not too thickly covered with hair. The tips of the ears should be pointed rather than round.

EYE SHAPE: The eye opening should be slightly almond-shaped.

BODY: The body should be medium to small in size; dainty, long, svelte, and graceful in outline and carriage. Neck should be long and slender.

TAIL: Tail should be long and tapering.

LEGS AND FEET: The legs should be proportionately long, slender, and small-boned, with hind legs slightly higher than front. Feet should be small and oval in shape.

COAT: The coat should be very dense, very short, lustrous, very fine-textured, soft, silky, and plushlike.

EYE COLOR: The color of the eyes should be as vividly green as possible.

COLOR: The color should be bright blue, even throughout and free from tabby shadings and markings. There are various shades of blue, but the lighter or lavender shade blue is preferred. No white is permissible.

CONDITION: GOOD PHYSICAL CONDITION.

SCALE OF POINTS

HEAD	10	LEGS AND FEET	10
EARS	5	COAT	15
EYE SHAPE	5	EYE COLOR	5
BODY	15	COLOR	20
TAIL	5	CONDITION	10
		TOTAL POINTS	100

KORAT STANDARD

HEAD: When viewed from the front, head is heart-shaped, with breadth between and across the eyes, gently curving to a well-developed, but not sharply pointed muzzle. Forehead, large flat. There is an indentation in the center of the forehead which accentuates this heart-shaped appearance. Strong chin and jaw. In profile there is a slight stop between forehead and nose. Nose is short and has a slight downward curve. Ears are large, with a rounded tip and large flair at base, set high on head, giving an alert expression. Inside ears sparsely furnished. Broad head, 5; profile, 6; breadth between eyes, 5; ear set and placement, 5.

BODY AND TAIL: Medium in size, with a strong, muscular, semi-cobby body; medium bone structure. The back is carried in a curve. Legs are well-proportioned to body; feet oval. The tail is medium in length, heavier at the base, tapering to a rounded tip. No penalty for imperfect tail. Body, 15; legs and feet, 5; tail, 5.

COLOR: Blue overall, tipped with silver, the more silver the better, without shading or tabby markings. Where the coat is short, the sheen of the silver is intensified. Paw pads dark blue, ranging to lavender with a pinkish tinge. Nose and lip leather is dark blue or lavender. Color, 20.

EYES: Large, luminous, are particularly prominent; wide open and oversized for the face. Eye aperture, which shows as well-rounded when fully open, has an Asian slant when closed or partially closed. Eye color: brilliant green preferred, amber cast acceptable. Allowance for kittens and adolescents. Color is not usually true until the cat is mature. Placement, 10; shape, 5; color, 5.

COAT: Single. Hair is short to medium in length, glossy and fine, lying close to the body. The coat over the spine is inclined to break as the cat moves. Short, 4; texture, 5; close lying, 2.

CONDITION: Perfect physical condition, muscular alert appearance.

MUST be registered N.C.A.F. Foundation record (F3) to be eligible to be shown in championship class. SIX (6) generations Korat to qualify for Studbook registration.

SCALE OF POINTS

COLOR	20	EYES (shape and placement)	15
HEAD (including ear set and placement)	20	COLOR	5
BODY AND TAIL	25	COAT	10
		CONDITION	5
		TOTAL POINTS	100

HAVANA BROWN STANDARD

HEAD: The head should be longer than it is wide, with a distinct "stop" at the eyes. The head narrows to a rounded muzzle, with a definite break behind the whiskers. Allowance for stud jowls and sparse furnishings on the lower lip.

WHISKERS: Brown. FAULT: White whiskers.

EARS: Ears are large, round-tipped, with very little hair inside or out, wide-set but not flaring.

EYES: Color should be chartreuse green, the greener shades preferred; shape should be oval.

BODY, NECK: Medium length, firm and muscular. Neck proportioned to the body. FAULT: Short neck or Siamese body type.

LEGS: Proportioned to the body. PAWS: oval.

TAIL: Medium in length in proportion to the body.
FAULTS: Thick, short, kinked, or Siamese type.

COAT: Must be medium length and smooth. FAULT:
Dull, open, or too close.

COLOR: A shade of rich, warm, mahogany brown.
Entire cat should be the same sound shade of brown to the
skin. Nose leather and paw pads must have rosy tone.
FAULTS: Any other than solid color. Black pads or nose
leather.

CONDITION: Firm and muscular. Coat must be glossy.
Eyes must be clear. FAULTS: Too fat or undernourished.

KITTENS: Allowance for Tabby markings or changing
eye color.

SCALE OF POINTS

HEAD	15	LEGS	10
WHISKERS	5	TAIL	5
EARS	5	COAT	15
EYES	10	COLOR	15
BODY AND		CONDITION	5
NECK	15		
		TOTAL POINTS	100

SIAMESE STANDARD

HEAD: The head should be long and well-proportioned,
narrowing in perfectly straight lines to a fine muzzle. A
wedge, as viewed from the front, is created by straight lines
from outer ear bases along sides of muzzle, without a break
in jaw line at the whiskers. Skull to be flat, and nose to be a
continuation of the forehead, with no break. In profile, a
straight line without a dip is seen from the center of the
forehead to tip of the nose and from tip of nose to chin.
Allowance to be made for jowls in stud cats. UNDESIR-
ABLE: Round or broad head; short or broad muzzle; bulging
forehead; receding chin; Roman nose.

EARS: Ears should be alert, rather large, wide at the
base, and pricked forward as though listening. OBJEC-

TIONS: Small or short ears; too much space between the ears; ears improperly set.

EYE SHAPE: The eye aperture should be almond-shaped, with an Oriental slant toward the nose. OBJEC-TIONS: Round or unslanted eye aperture; crossed eyes.

BODY TYPE: Medium in size, long, lithe, and svelte. Overall body structure to be fine-boned and firmly muscled. OBJECTIONS: Cobby or short, thick body.

NECK: The neck should be long and slender. OBJEC-TIONS: Short or thick neck.

TAIL: Tail should be narrow at the base, long and tapering, and without visible kink. OBJECTIONS: Short thick tail; winners to be withheld for a visible misplacement or abnormality of any joint in the tail.

LEGS AND FEET: Legs proportionately slim and long enough to carry the body length gracefully; hind legs slightly higher than front. Feet small and oval in shape. OBJEC-TIONS: Short legs; heavy leg bones; large or round feet. Withhold winners for white toes.

COAT: The coat should be very short and fine in texture, glossy, and close-lying. OBJECTIONS: Rough, shaggy, or coarse coat.

EYE COLOR: Eyes should be clear, brilliant, and of a deep blue color.

BODY COLOR: The body color should be even, with slightly darker shading across the shoulders and back, shading gradually into lighter color on belly and chest; darker coloring allowed for older cats; kittens lighter in color generally. OBJECTIONS: uneven body color or shading; dark spots on belly; Tabby or ticked markings.

POINTS: The mask, ears, legs, and tail should be clearly defined in darker shade. Except in kittens, the mask and ears should be connected by tracings. OBJECTIONS: Complete hood; light hairs in points; bars on the tail.

CONDITION: Hard and muscular, with no indication of fat.

OBJECTION: Emaciation due to underfeeding.

SCALE OF POINTS

HEAD:			
Profile	3		
Wedge	5		
Chin	2		
	—	10	
EARS		5	
EYE SHAPE		10	
BODY TYPE		7	
NECK		3	
TAIL		5	
LEGS AND FEET		5	
		—	
TOTAL POINTS FOR TYPE		45	
COAT:			
Closeness of Coat	5		
Shortness of Coat	5		
	—	10	
EYE COLOR		10	

BODY COLOR:			
Tone and depth			
of color	5		
Shading	5		
	—	10	
POINTS:			
Depth of color	5		
Evenness of Color	5		
Conformation to			
Pattern	5		
	—	15	
TOTAL POINTS FOR COAT			
AND COLOR		45	
CONDITION		10	
		—	
TOTAL POINTS		100	

SIAMESE COLORS

FROST POINT: The body of the Frost Point Siamese should be an even milk-white color. The points should be a frost gray of pinkish tone; the dilute pigment permitting the flesh tone to show through, resulting in a delicate peach-blossom tone of the inner surface of the ears, while the foot pads have a coral-pink color, and the nose leather presents a translucent old lilac hue at the tip. The eyes should be a brilliant blue, the deeper shade preferred. Matching nose leather and paw pads preferred.

BLUE POINT: The body of the Blue Point should be a glacial white, shading into the same gray-blue tone as the points, but of a lighter shade. Points should be platinum gray of bluish tone, and the color of all points should be as nearly the same tone as possible. Eyes should be a brilliant blue, the deeper tones preferred. Matching blue nose leather and paw pads preferred. UNDESIRABLE: Fawn or cream shadings.

CHOCOLATE POINT: The body of the Chocolate Point should be an ivory color all over with shadings, if any, to be in the color of the points. The points should be a warm milk-chocolate color; the ears, mask, legs, paws, and tail to be as even in color as possible. The ears should not be darker than the other points. Matching milk-chocolate nose leather and paw pads preferred. Eyes should be a brilliant blue, deeper tones preferred. UNDESIRABLE: Exhibits with dark intensity of tone of foot pads and the tip of the nose leather, as seen in Seal Point Siamese, shall be disqualified for competition in Chocolate Point Classes.

SEAL POINT: The body of the Seal Point Siamese should be an even pale fawn or cream, shading gradually into a lighter color on the belly and chest. Points should be a dense, deep, seal brown, all points being of the same shade. Eyes brilliant blue, deeper shades preferred. Matching nose leather and paw pads preferred. UNDESIRABLE: Black or gray shading.

RED POINT: The body color should be a creamy white, with shadings, if at all, of dilute red in the same tone as the points. The points should be red; the deeper the shade the better. Since red is a slowly developing, reduced-color pigment, two years should be allowed for full-color intensity to develop in the points. Kittens should be white in body color, with deeper cream points. Eyes should be a brilliant blue, the deeper shades preferred. Salmon-pink matching nose leather and paw pads preferred.

ALBINO: Body color should be a solid white. No color in the points; point allotment 25. Eyes should be clear pink, with blue showing through. Point allotment 10. OBJECTIONS: Pale, milky, gray, yellowish, or dark blue tinge.

TORTIE POINT: Masks and points must conform to color standard.

REX STANDARD

HEAD: Should be longer than it is wide, with a break at the muzzle when viewed from the front, and a Roman profile. From the top of the nose to the chin should be a straight line.

NECK: Should be medium long and slender.

EARS: Should be large and naked, set high on the head, taller than they are wide, with a modified point at the tip.

EYES: Should be medium in size, oval in shape. A color in keeping with the coat color is desirable, but is secondary to overall appearance of the eyes.

TAIL: Should be long and slender, tapering slightly from the body to the end. It is sometimes tipped with a tuft of waves. There is no penalty for a bare upper surface.

BODY: Should be long, slender, with "tuck-up" behind the ribs, and hips somewhat heavy in proportion to the rest of the body. Body must be hard and muscular, medium to small in size, with fine bones.

LEGS: Should be long and slender, in keeping with type of body and tail. A Rex cat is high on the legs, with feet that are dainty.

COAT: Is very fine and very soft. Coat should be short and dense. A coat with deep, even waves is desirable, especially on the back and tail. Coat on head and legs shall be texture of velvet pile.

COLOR AND MARKINGS: As for Manx Cat.

CONDITION: Firm and muscular. Lack of condition shows in flabbiness, loss of coat quality, and dull look in eyes. Disposition should be calm. Viewed as a whole, the cat shall be well-knit, smooth, with each part in good proportion.

DISQUALIFICATION: Presence of any coarse or guard hairs.

SCALE OF POINTS

HEAD:				
Shape, muzzle break	5		TUCK-UP	5
Profile	3		LEGS	5
Chin	2		COAT:	
SUBTOTAL	—	10	Texture	10
			Density	10
NECK	5		Waviness	10
EARS	5			—	30
EYES	5		COLOR AND MARKINGS	10
TAIL	5		CONDITION	5
BODY	10		BALANCE	5
			TOTAL POINTS	**100**

A Tabby and Seal-point kittens. (From *The Arco Book of Cats* by Grace Pond, photo by Anne Cumbers.)

Whether at rest or in motion, cats exhibit a natural grace that is unequaled by any other animal.

CHAPTER ELEVEN

ACCIDENTS AND FIRST AID

ON THE WHOLE, I don't think you can describe cats as being accident prone. They are more delicate and less blundering in their movements than dogs. You can't imagine a dog walking among ornaments and not knocking any over, but a cat treads with exquisite care.

Road Accidents

The most common form of accident these days is for the cat to be hit by a car, or actually run over. There is only one thing that can be done if the cat is obviously badly hurt or unconscious and that is to very carefully slide a blanket or something similar beneath it and carry it to some quiet place. Warmth is the important thing, and the animal should be well-covered and watched over until the vet arrives. The quieter it is kept and the less it is handled until the expert arrives the better, for obvious reasons.

If it is so badly hurt that the vet can do nothing to save it, he will put it painlessly to sleep. It is to be hoped that the day that ignorant and callous people destroy cats by drowning, whether injured or not, is over.

Drowning

There are occasions when cats fall into a well or some other water from which they cannot escape, and if they are rescued in time, it is sometimes possible to revive them by artificial respiration. Life may appear to be extinct, but there is always hope. First of all, hold the animal's head down so as to free the lungs of liquid. Then lay it down on its right side. Now gently press the palms of your hands on the ribs and exert pressure. Relax, exert again, and so on until air is pumped into the lungs and breathing begins or hope is gone. If you have been successful, get the cat dry as quickly as you possibly can by briskly rubbing with dry towels.

Traps

The cat is seldom an easy creature to deal with when it is hurt. Even the most gentle ones will panic and scratch and bite at the hands which are trying to minister to them. If you ever do come across a cat in a steel trap, and I most sincerely hope you will not, there is only one thing to do and that is to throw your coat over it. Keeping the cat tightly bundled in your arms, you will be able to release it by pressing your foot or knee on the spring.

Any animal that gets caught in these awful things is usually dreadfully mangled and only a vet will be able to tell you whether the poor creature can be saved or not.

Poisoning

If your cat is in pain and vomiting and you suspect that it may have picked up poison, give it a universal antidote at once and following the instructions on the label, send for the vet without delay.

Overcome By Fumes

It is a rare thing for cats to be gassed, but they have been known to be overcome from car fumes in the garage. Get them into the fresh air with all possible speed and use artificial respiration, as described for drowning.

Hair Balls

Cats who lick their coats a lot sometimes regurgitate pellets of fur. When a cat eats grass, it usually indicates that he has this condition. There is nothing to be alarmed about, for this seems to be quite a natural function with cats, particularly the long-haired variety. You could, however, regard it as a hint that a little extra grooming would not be amiss. A little medicinal paraffin will help free the cat of this trouble. Femalt, given as directed, aids both the elimination and prevention of hair balls.

Fishhooks and Bones

It is quite a common thing for a cat to get a piece of bone wedged crosswise in the roof of its mouth. It happens to dogs as well. It is a good idea not to let cats eat very small bones. Although the piece of bone is probably not hurting the animal, the fact that it is there seems to cause a panicky reaction. You therefore need to act as swiftly as you can. The first indication of the trouble is clawing at the mouth and rubbing the sides of the jaw on the ground. There will probably be frothing at the mouth also.

Imprison the cat's body and legs tightly in a towel; then place a hand over the top of the head, opening the jaws with a finger and thumb. Draw the head back, and you will see the obstruction high in the roof of the mouth. The handle of a spoon, with the curve following the curve of the mouth, is an excellent tool to dislodge the piece of bone.

It is a very good idea to practice opening your pet's jaw once or twice just to get the knack. Then, if the emergency should arise, you should be able to remove the obstacle in a few seconds after noticing the condition. The quicker you are, the less frightened your pet will be and the less resistance you will encounter.

It sometimes happens that a sharp fish bone becomes embedded in some part of the mouth. The drill system is the same except that a pair of forceps or tweezers will be the tool to use. It is always better, obviously, if you have someone to hold the cat while you investigate the mouth, but it can be done singlehandedly. I find the best way is to sit in a chair so that I can use my knees and body to help restrain any struggles.

I hope your cat is never unlucky enough to have a fishhook lodged in its mouth. But it does happen sometimes. Unless you are a very practical and cool person, you will be best advised to rush the animal straight to a vet. Again, the greater the delay, the more terrified the cat will become. If the hook is in an easy place to get at, such as the lip, the best way is to push the hook further in, until the barb emerges. Then sever the shank of the hook with a pair of pliers so as to remove the loop, and it can then be drawn out quite easily. If the barb is embedded, never attempt to pull it out the way it went in. You will make a nasty wound instead of a small puncture.

Whether bone or fishhook, if it is awkwardly positioned and there is the possibility of the layman making the wound and the pain worse, the best policy is to whisk the cat off to the vet with as little delay as possible.

Stings and Bites

It is not an unusual thing for a cat to be stung by a wasp or bee. They usually ask for this treatment by playing with the insect, not being aware, of course, of its means of re-taliation. The sting of the bee is usually left in the victim, and this should be removed and the wound rubbed with a paste made with baking soda. A wasp usually goes away with its sting, and the wound that it makes should be bathed in vinegar. If you have not actually witnessed the stinging, your only indication for treatment will be whether the sting is left in the wound or not.

Directly after a sting, the cat will be in a panic and will no doubt indicate the position of the wound by some action, such as shaking its paw or its head.

There is always the chance of a country cat being bitten by a poisonous snake. If the bite is on a limb, and it nearly always is, place a tourniquet above the bite and call a vet.

Treatment after Accident

The one golden rule to observe following an accident of any kind to your cat is to keep it warm and as quiet as possible. Cats are sensitive creatures, and they do suffer from shock.

CHAPTER TWELVE

CATS AS COMPANIONS

AFTER THE LISTING of all these various breeds of cats, I must confess that if I were only to be allowed to keep one, there would be no hesitation on my part. It would be a Siamese. To me, they are the most beautiful of all cats to look at and the most interesting in character.

Yet all cats seem to have characters of their own. Cats of the same breed might be expected to behave and react in the same way. But they do not, wherein lies much of their charm and fascination.

Every kitten born of a humble alley cat is different when it becomes adult. They may feed the same way, hunt the same way, and probably court the same way, but there is always something different about each one of them.

I knew one female cat of humble and nondescript breed who had such a strong maternal instinct that she suckled a newborn rabbit. This came about because a dog dug out a doe's nesting hole and chewed up all the young but one. The rabbit was found alive and uninjured among the remains of the nest. It was given to the cat as an experiment and a consolation because her litter had been taken away and destroyed.

Although this cat was a good hunter, she took to the blind and furless creature and never showed it anything but affection, even when it grew up and really looked, and one supposes, smelled like a rabbit. On the other hand, you have the antithesis in the cat mentioned earlier who took no interest in her brood and never even troubled to find a nest for them.

Then again, I have a Siamese who hardly talks at all. She utters the typical deep-throated Siamese cry when she is hungry or wants to be let out, but that is all. But there is another who will talk tirelessly—not because he wants something, but just to be friendly. Take him for a walk in the garden and he will keep close by your feet and talk away in answer to anything you say to him. And that deep Siamese voice from low down in his chest really does sound like talking.

Siamese are what you might call matey and affectionate as a rule. But like any other cat, or like dogs, their nature is molded to a great extent when they are young. A puppy that is continually teased will probably grow into a bad-tempered dog and a real danger. And who can blame it? It is just the same with kittens. They quite naturally respond to thought and kindness and thus grow into gentle and interesting cats. There are spiteful cats, but I don't think it is born in them:

Talking about different temperaments in cats, there is a mongrel cat belonging to a friend who likes to take a flying leap onto his back, climb to his shoulders, and go for a ride around the garden. This was regarded as an endearing habit, and not one to be discouraged, until one blazing summer day when this gentleman sauntered into the garden minus his shirt!

Among his other cats, he has another with an unusual trait. If this one is given a little smack for being naughty, such as for stealing someone else's food, he immediately turns and attacks the nearest cat to him in no uncertain manner.

All cats seem to like pretending, and Siamese enjoy this game even more than most. I have one that pretends to be afraid occasionally. It's just a game really. She adores every member of the family, but sometimes she tries to give the impression that she has been naughty (which she never is) and dashes under the sofa as soon as you enter the room. After a minute or so, a small head will appear from under the frill, those vivid blue eyes will meet yours for a moment, and the head will be hurriedly withdrawn. What you are supposed to do now is lie down and start groping under the sofa. Not likely!

There is only one way. Completely ignore her, and she will be up on your knees in a short time, demanding attention.

She seems to like this "pretending-I've-been-naughty" game best if you happen to come on the scene when she is near the back door. Then she's off, up the garden path as fast as she can go, with her back end swerving to one side, independent of the front. She so manages to convince herself that she is in real trouble, if not deadly danger, that all her fur gets ruffled. When she reaches the bottom of the garden, she flings herself up the trunk of a small tree and sits on a limb, lashing her tail to and fro. You feel rather ashamed that you did not further the burlesque by chasing after her roaring blood-curdling threats as you ran.

Then there is the game of pretending to be a ferocious panther, or some other savage jungle beast. She might be sitting on a warm patch of the flower border when a moth settles on the lawn. Then what a change of expression! Gone is the dreamy look from her innocent blue eyes. Now they seem to stab with the intensity of their concentration. The tail lashes. Then follows the deadly, belly-creeping stalk across the lawn.

The fact that the grass has only just been cut, and is hardly an inch high, does not stop her from acting as if she were taking advantage of every piece of cover. But, of course, it's elephant grass really, and the moth is a young deer or a hare.

What a vicious-looking beast she has suddenly become! Ears tucked back, tail quivering slightly, she would like to lash it thoroughly, but is afraid to attract attention. The nearer she gets to the moth (or deer) the more the spirits of her ancestors seem to take over. Her expression becomes absolutely venomous. Now she is within pouncing distance. Very carefully she moves her body and limbs into the right position for launching. She nearly went then, but checked herself. The moment is so exquisite she must linger another few seconds.

For a few more moments she glares at her prey. Real jungle stuff this. Then she cannot restrain herself another moment and the slender body is catapulted through the air. But it is too late. The moth has taken wing. She flings herself high in the air, with unsheathed front claws grasping, but misses by inches.

The next moment she is walking sedately back across the lawn with all trace of blood lust and savagery wiped from her face. The usual look of kittenish innocence is in its place.

I have noticed that those people who talk to their cats a lot seem to bring much more out of their pets. To non-cat lovers it may seem silly and childish perhaps, but I know one tough ex-navy man who quite unashamedly chats away to his cat, and it really appears as if the animal understands quite a lot. This one has acquired the habit of going upstairs every morning at six thirty, jumping on the bed, and tapping his master gently on the cheek until he wakes. This happens almost to the minute every morning. The only time the ritual is interrupted is when the clocks are altered, his master tells me. But routine is resumed normally within a day or two.

Personally I would be inclined to "set" this feline alarm for somewhere more in the region of eight thirty!

The same gentleman told me another story about this particular animal. One winter evening he was peeling onions for pickling. He was sitting close to the fire and putting the onions as he peeled them into a bowl at his feet. The cat, of course, was also close to the fire. When presently the owner looked down, he saw the cat first wiping one eye with a paw and then the other. It stood it as long as it could, being reluctant to leave the fire, but eventually retired to the other side of the room with tears still streaming down and wetting the fur of its cheeks.

In conclusion, I would reiterate to the new owner of a young kitten that all that is needed to train it to become scrupulously clean is a little patience. Everything is on your side in this matter, because cats are naturally very particular animals, and a tiny kitten, only just beginning to run about, can be quickly trained. It *wants* to be clean.

There is just one other thing to save anxiety. If your kitten is female and you have her spayed, you may be as shocked as I was the first time I saw one after the operation. For one thing, the fur is shaved from the flank and the incision is quite a large one, calling for a number of stitches. It may look to you, as I remember it looked to me, as if the kitten's appearance has been ruined for life. But don't worry. In a few weeks, when the fur has grown again, you would never know that an operation had been carried out. She may be feeling very sorry for herself for a day or two, but keep her warm and quiet and she will soon be fit and playful again.

. Whether your kitten be male or female, pedigree or mongrel, I hope it will give you many years of companionship, affection, and entertainment, and that something of what you have read in these pages may have helped to bring this about.